GW00836624

TELLING TALES

AN ORAL HISTORY OF DUBAI

Telling Tales: An Oral History of Dubai
1st Edition December 2005
Reprint August 2010

Text
Julia Wheeler

Photography
Paul Thuysbaert

Published By
Explorer Publishing & Distribution
PO Box 34275, Dubai, UAE
Phone (+971-4) 340 8805
Fax (+971-4) 340 8806
www.explorerpublishing.com

ISBN 976-8182-64-4

© Explorer Publishing & Distribution 2005, 2010
Text © Julia Wheeler 2005
Photography © Paul Thuysbaert 2005
Old photographs © individual storytellers

Colour separations – Emirates Printing Press
Printing – Emirates Printing Press

All rights reserved. No part of this publication may be reproduced, stored in a retrieval system or transmitted, in any form or by any means, electronic, mechanical, photocopying, recording or otherwise, except brief extracts for the purpose of review, without the prior permission in writing of the publisher and copyright owner.

TELLING TALES

AN ORAL HISTORY OF DUBAI

JULIA WHEELER & PAUL THUYSBAERT

EXPLORER

For Alfred and Edie, Betty and John – my grandparents.
Your stories of horses and carts, war-time fire engines, Land Girls'
adventures and the Rat and Sparrow Club will always be magical for me.

JW

To my children, Ray and Aaron and their mother, my wife, Kirtie.
Also to my mother, Ray, and my father, Osmond, who also had stories,
sadly no longer to be told. My greatest respect goes to them.

PT

And to Laura Jayne Snelling, a good friend and
dedicated wife and mother who would have smiled at these tales of the
place she and her family enjoyed together.

PT and JW

CONTENTS

INTRODUCTION

Slipping off my shoes, pushing the door ajar and walking hesitantly into the Fishermen's Majlis near the beach in Umm Suqeim, my heart was thumping. While driving there I'd repeated aloud, in undoubtedly poor Arabic, what I knew I needed to say to have any chance of getting what I wanted.

"My name's Julia Wheeler, I work for the BBC in London. I've lived here ten years – with my husband – and I'm writing a book about the history of Dubai. I would like to talk to someone who used to be a pearl diver."

Reciting my piece for real I made sure it was loud enough for all the men in their pristine white *kandouras* to hear. They pretended not to listen as they sat in groups on the floor playing cards or dominos, but I could tell they were curious. It didn't take long before I was directed to a tall, thin, dignified elder sitting quietly to the side of the room with his friends. Bilal Khamis gestured for some Arabic coffee and we sat together – both of us smiling nervously while exchanging copious Arabic pleasantries. I had found my pearl diver.

So began, for me, one of the most crucial interviews in this book – after all, how could An Oral History of Dubai not include someone involved in the business which sustained the town for so long? Hence my thumping heart. I would have begged to hear the stories, but I didn't need to – they were willingly recalled and shared.

Like all the people in this book, Bilal had no real reason to talk to me. To him, as to many others included within these pages, I was a stranger, an unknown entity; someone who may or may not tell things as they really were.

I need not have worried; the generous welcome both Paul and I received in return for our intrigue with Dubai's past was repeated over and over throughout the city – in homes, *majlis's*, offices, farms, a doctor's surgery, a boatyard and a police station.

Since beginning the book we have heard of the youthful escapades and adventures of some of the most respected members of Dubai's society. Paul has had the privilege of capturing the character and essence of Emiratis who've never allowed their pictures to appear in public before. I've held hands with ladies I'd only just met as they told stories not spoken in years and while tears gathered in their eyes, and mine.

People have been trusting with their memories – memories that are personal and precious. In return I have promised that the stories shared will be portrayed as they were told – in word and in spirit.

Storytelling in Arabian societies is part of history itself. As well as adding to the entertainment around an evening campfire, for centuries it was one of the ways through which knowledge, mores and a sense of belonging were preserved across the generations, helping to create strong and often vital bonds.

In writing 'Telling Tales' I have tried to bear this in mind. The tales are written from the words and stories as they were told to me. Arabic words are explained in the glossary. The stories are not always verbatim simply for ease of reading, but each tale is written with the conversational style of the individual in mind and with their recorded words playing back in my ears.

I believe this combination, together with the insightful and well-observed portraits, provides a flavour of the spirit and nature of each individual and enables his or her personality to come alive and jump from the page.

The oral history of any country allows a glimpse at 'ordinary' lives by going deeper than the accepted record of events – almost certainly written by 'the winners'. Such history is not the 'official' version and is often so much more engaging precisely because of that.

Dubai is the perfect hunting ground for oral historians – even people who grew up in the city in the 1950s and 1960s have fascinating stories to tell about the changes they've witnessed. Listening to tales from the 1920s and 1930s I now know that those recounting them inhabited a different world altogether.

Of course, oral history relies on people's memories and perceptions – past and present. As with any account, the events of the past are viewed through the eyes, and with the attitudes, of more recent times. People are selective in what they remember and what they would like to be known by others. Inevitably stories were relayed after the microphone had been switched off – stories too personal or too sensitive to be told here.

The subjects people didn't want to speak of are as significant as the ones they were happy to share. Many were not keen to dwell on the so-called 'gold smuggling' era in the Gulf in the 1950s and 1960s, perhaps fearing that it's not quite ancient history yet. In another generation it may become something to talk of more openly – much like how the 18th and 19th Century smuggling along Britain's south coast is now celebrated and incorporated proudly into the region's heritage. Having a 'gold smuggler' as a great-grandfather could become an open badge of honour; many stories of those times are undoubtedly already recounted fondly in the privacy of today's Emirati gatherings – around the campfire or otherwise.

This book does not pretend to be an academic work, but Paul and I believe it does give a unique insight into a time and place from which stories like these would be better re-told rather than lost forever.

Both Paul's children and mine were born in Dubai. As they grow up in this high-rise, fast-moving, modern metropolis, it's natural to wonder if they will be able to believe that these tales happened not in some far off land, but in a place which shares the same name and geography as Dubai.

Julia Wheeler, Dubai

HISTORICAL CONTEXT

If Dubai's history over the last century or so was to be summed up in a single phrase, that phrase might be, "As one door closed, another one opened". The notion is also reflected in the lives of the people who inhabited the village, town or city as it grew.

Long before oil was discovered off the shores of the southern Gulf, a precious commodity of a different type was sought beneath the waves. Diving for pearls is believed to have been steadily underway during the 1700s, but the General Peace Treaty of 1820 between the British and the leaders of the newly defined 'Trucial Coast' made for greater political, social and economic stability. Pearling flourished and with it the lives of many people in settlements along the coast improved to some degree. Although the nomadic lifestyle continued for some until the second half of the 20th Century, it was 100 years before that Bedouin tribes began to migrate from the desert to the coast foregoing their transient past in favour of a more settled, and arguably more comfortable, life.

Pearl diving was vital to the economy of the Trucial Coast. The annual summer dive took most able-bodied men and older boys away from Dubai for several months. 'The Dive' touched every family in some way because it was the only means for many to earn the money they needed to live; their share of the catch effectively had to sustain them for the rest of the year. Many people found themselves in a precarious situation living hand to mouth, year to year. So developed a complex economic and social interdependence which was based upon the diving, but which came also to dictate relationships on dry land. Those who went to sea each year are only part of the story and often found themselves near the bottom of the pearling hierarchy. Complicated bonds of allegiance and debt were forged between divers, boat captains, boat owners and the different strands of pearl merchants. Some merchants went to sea themselves while the wealthiest enjoyed the privilege of waiting for the fruits of the catch to be brought back to them on the shore.

Payment would be advanced in order to fit out the boats, sustain the families of the divers during the diving season or make-up the shortfall in earnings from a previous year's disappointing catch. In the lustrous years of pearling, there was money to be made and people lived relatively well, but when the catch was poor – perhaps because of bad weather or disease onboard the boats – the whole economy of Dubai suffered as there was nothing to fall back on. Many of the people whose stories are included in this book either took part in pearling themselves or remember their fathers, uncles, brothers and friends being involved. Their personal stories mainly come from the end of the prosperous years of pearling, but they remember the tales of when pearls had meant significant wealth for some in Dubai and along the Trucial Coast.

The start of the door being closed on the pearling era had come just as at it had reached its peak in the Gulf – at the end of the 1920s. The hardships of the worldwide economic depression that followed were made worse in this region by the increasingly widespread availability of Japanese cultured pearls. The value of natural pearls in the Gulf's traditional markets had fallen dramatically and with it so had the incomes of those reliant on pearling. Nevertheless, it seems a sizeable pearling fleet continued to put to sea until the middle of the 20th Century simply because there were few alternatives for earning money to live.

The pearling boats were used for fishing in the winter months and during this impoverished time some were converted for use as trading vessels, sailing the waters of the Gulf, the Arabian Sea and the Indian Ocean with their cargos of dates, rice, cloth and other goods.

Traders had been travelling to and from Persia for many years, but towards the end of the 19th Century, the authorities controlling the port of Lingah increased taxes and so the merchants who had traded from there wanted to find a different base for their business. Many were from Bastak and they were invited to settle in Dubai – in the area which was to become known as Bastakia – by the then ruler, Sheikh Maktoum bin Hasher. Resident himself in Shindagha, he was part of the dynasty which had broken away from Abu Dhabi 60 years earlier and, together with around 800 followers, had moved (as it was to transpire) permanently to the tiny, and at that time unimportant, village of Dubai.

Partly as a result of the movement south by merchants from the northern shores of the Gulf, Dubai became a centre for trade which was only to increase in the century which followed. Ironically, after the depression of the 1930s, it was the ravages of the Second World War which brought relief to some in Dubai in the form of rations from the British Government. Food and supplies that exceeded requirements were bought by some enterprising merchants and smuggled over the water into Iran, bringing money back into Dubai.

Since the discovery of oil in Kuwait and Saudi Arabia in the late 1930s, some people from Dubai had decided to seek their fortunes in countries which neighboured the Trucial Coast. These economic migrants would send money back home to support their families and they often had specific financial targets in mind – earning enough money to get married or to start a business.

It was around this time that the man who is so often called the Father of Dubai came further to the fore. Working under the leadership of his father, Sheikh Saeed, until 1958 and later as ruler in his own right, Sheikh Rashid is widely credited by both friend and foe with changing the face of the town to which he was so devoted. The dredging of The Creek at the end of the 1950s, the establishment of modern institutions of government and public services as well as huge infrastructure projects in the 1960s and 1970s all opened the door to new opportunities for Dubai and its people.

One of the most controversial periods of Dubai's past was the export of gold from the city which later found its way to India. Opinions differed on the legalities of the practice depending on which side of the Arabian Sea they were viewed from. It was perfectly lawful for people to buy gold in Dubai and export it. The controversy arose – and lives on – because it was illegal to import gold into India. There was huge demand for the precious metal there and the incentive for smuggling was high. The rewards from this were brought back to the Gulf in the form of rupees and subsequently officially repatriated in exchange for pounds sterling. Effectively the Indian government was having to pay for illegally-imported gold with its foreign exchange reserves – something which came as a double blow.

India's withdrawal of its currency from the Gulf in an attempt to halt what it saw as gold smuggling coincided with Dubai's discovery of oil. This precious commodity from the sea – which, as popular legend would have it, was often found in the same areas as the best pearling locations – allowed the continuation, albeit at a faster pace, of what had already been initiated in terms of investment and development. The oil wealth was used to supplement what Dubai knew best – trade.

The creation of the United Arab Emirates in 1971 was to bring greater stability and fuel further growth in Dubai. By then a city, Dubai was able to keep its position as the pre-eminent trading centre along southern Gulf shores. For women in particular the creation of a union meant previously unheard of work and career possibilities.

Dubai has, by necessity, been in the position of having to reinvent itself and its economic life over and over again in the space of the past century. The histories told in this book are testament to that. This may go some way towards explaining why Dubai always seems determined to discover 'the next big thing' – that resourcefulness has ensured survival in the past and by the same logic, many would argue, it is what will ensure the city continues to thrive in the future. After all, the only constant in Dubai is change.

AUTHOR'S NOTE

Modern Arabic spellings have been used and the punctuation employed to define Arabic letters for which there are no English equivalents has been dropped.

The names of those interviewed and spoken of are written as the storytellers wished them to appear. Some have relatives' and tribal names included, others do not.

Inconsistencies in the use of words (such as 'Al' before place names) have been retained because they represent the different spoken styles of the storytellers. Around half of the chapters were translated from the Arabic at the time the stories were told, by people close to and trusted by the subject.

Although individuals from many nationalities undoubtedly have significant stories to tell about Dubai's history, the scope of the book was deliberately limited to Emiratis – the people of Dubai telling their own story. They were chosen for their knowledge and experience of the subjects upon which they speak.

PHOTOGRAPHER'S NOTE

All the portraits of the storytellers were taken with the world's first integrated medium-format digital camera, the Hasselblad H1D camera with a 22 megapixel sensor. They were taken mostly outdoors during Dubai's summer months, using portable studio lighting.

NOTE ON CURRENCIES

Maria Theresa dollars and gold coins were highly prized and widely in circulation along the Trucial Coast, but because of historical trading links with the Indian Subcontinent, in the early and middle part of the 20th Century the main trading currency became the Indian rupee. The illegal importation of gold into India in the 1950's, and the subsequent exchange of rupees earned in this trade for foreign exchange, prompted the Indian government to introduce the distinct (and different coloured) Gulf rupees in 1959. The continued import of gold to India saw rupees withdrawn altogether from use in the southern Gulf by the end of 1966. Dubai briefly adopted the Saudi riyal, followed by the Qatar and Dubai riyal and later, after federation, the UAE dirham.

CHAPTER 1

The Learned Man

SHEIKH OMAR OBAID AL MAJID AL MUHAIRI

TRANSLATED BY FAMILY FRIEND, OSMAN HASSAN YOUSIF ABURUF

Dubai, like many places, started as a small town. At the time I was born in 1930 there were only a few buildings built of stone – most houses, especially around Bur Dubai, were made of dried palm fronds and called *khaimahs*. Our house, however, was made of stone. It was in the heart of the city in the area called Al Budoor – on Deira side near where the Gold Souq is now. At that time all the people lived around The Creek because life was based there.

Life was so simple – not like now. Back then, the main business was pearling and people used to go to sea to dive for the pearls which would be sold in India and then sent to Paris. Pearling time was between June and September and everyone was involved. The sea was warm during these months. This meant education happened only in the winter because people were earning their living in the summer. My father, Obaid Majid Mohammed Suroor, worked in pearling. He was the *nokhada* of his own diving boat. There were around 30 people on his boat. He was a learned and a devout man.

'I believe this is the only part of the world where pearling was taught in the classroom.'

At that time education was in private hands and the ruler was not involved because there wasn't enough money to spend on education. Instead, business people co-operated with the ruler over education. The first school in Dubai, Al Ahmadiya, was established by Sheikh Ahmad bin Dalmook (1), who was a very rich man.

I entered Al Ahmadiya School at the age of six. Education at that time was based on teaching Arabic, Islam and some Mathematics. The other subject that was particular to the area was pearling. We were taught the business of pearling – the types of pearls, how to value them, which would sell for the best price, which were no good and so on. This was the most important topic which was beyond traditional education. I believe this is the only part of the world where pearling was taught in the classroom.

In those days children were quiet and innocent. We were hungry for knowledge so we were interested and very keen to learn. We were not aiming to get a certificate in order to get a job! I was in Al Ahmadiya until I was 16 years old and then, because there were very few resources at that time, I became a teacher there for four years. Afterwards I went to study in Mecca in Saudi Arabia. I remember it was 1369 in the Hijri calendar. (2) At the Grand Mosque I had a very good chance of a good education. I studied business transactions, rules of marriage and divorce, inheritance and so on.

After six years I was on a visit to Dubai before going back to start work at a primary school in Mecca. I went to see Sheikh Rashid and he told me, "You are welcome back." I told him my plans and he told me, "In Mecca they will find another teacher, but here we are badly in need of your

services." Before the Second World War there were only a few schools in Dubai – like Al Ahmadiya and Al Falah. However, after the war, people wanted more education so more schools were built.

Sheikh Rashid at that time had moved to Zabeel. He told me he didn't want his sons to have to cross The Creek to the Deira side for their education and so we would need a school on the Bur Dubai side. It was called Al Saeediya School (3) and was between Al Rifaa and Shindagha. He said I would teach his sons there, so I taught Sheikh Maktoum, Sheikh Hamdan and Sheikh Mohammed – Sheikh Ahmed bin Rashid was too young at that time.

At Al Saeediya there were classrooms with blackboards and tables and chairs.

There was no uniform – everybody wore what they normally wore and still they are doing that in the schools here. Back then though education was only for boys. We had two shifts; morning from eight to twelve noon and then the pupils came back from four to six.

As well as being a teacher and helping to organise the schools in Dubai, as a religious sheikh I was also given absolute power by Sheikh Rashid to conduct marriages. In Islam, marriage is in the hands of the ruler, but he gives powers to people to work on his behalf. I was the one to commission the Maktoum family's marriages. Marriage was family-arranged so when the families had approved of the choice my role began. I would know who was divorced, who was a virgin, who was widowed and so on and I settled the dowry according to these things.

Then there would be a big party at the bride's home with songs and celebrations – usually it went on for three days.

In 1960 the Land Department was founded by Sheikh Rashid and Sheikh Maktoum was the head of it. I was called in by Sheikh Rashid. He told me, "Omar, finish, you have to stop education now – I am giving you another job." I told him I was happy being a teacher because in that profession nobody hurt me and I didn't hurt anybody. In the Land Department there was value for people and I felt where there was money involved people might blame me for some situations, so I told him I didn't want to take this job. I believe Sheikh Rashid trusted me deeply. He said "Omar, no. I will never accept your apology on this, you must take the job." I obeyed him.

During this work I had difficulties with big and powerful people in Dubai and there were some problems, but if anyone had a complaint against me I asked that Sheikh Rashid would call us both together – sometimes people used to run away from the *majlis* when they saw me coming! Sheikh Rashid was such a simple, modest man. We could be very frank, open and outspoken with him. Later, he told me I was right to ask him to listen to both sides.

'I had a close relationship with Sheikh Rashid – I know things nobody else knows.'

I had a close relationship with Sheikh Rashid – I know things nobody else knows. He worked very hard for the development of Dubai. He helped the poor and worked late at night for the good of the city. He helped people in a very generous way and he was a devout Muslim in all his transactions. When I was leading the final prayer at the death of Sheikh Rashid, I remembered his dedication to Dubai, his keenness, his good behaviour and his modesty. I almost fainted with emotion while praying for his soul.

Sheikh Omar lives surrounded by his family in Al Mezhar in Dubai.

He was photographed at Al Ahmadiya School.

1. 1912.
2. 1949 or 1950 in the Gregorian calendar. The Hijri calendar started in the moon year in which the Prophet Mohammed migrated from Mecca to Medina.
3. Named after Sheikh Saeed.

CHAPTER 2

The Pearl Diver

BILAL KHAMIS

TRANSLATED BY HIS FRIENDS, MOHAMMED AL MARZOUQI AND MOHAMMED K. AL ROUM

I was born in Jumeirah – I don't know when. I am 60, 65, 70, 80 – I don't know. My father was a pearl diver. In Jumeirah there was only desert, nothing else at all. No cars, nothing. If we wanted to go to the market we had to walk. Only the sheikhs had a car back then.

Pearl diving happened in summer and lasted for around three months. The number of people on the boats depended on the size of the boat. Some had 15, 20, 30 – up to 60 people if it was a big boat. On my boat there were between 35 and 40 people. I went diving on the same *nokhada's* boat each year. The *nokhada* would engage us in the winter and give us money. He would give each person 15 or 20 rupees to buy rice, sugar, whatever, for the family for three months while we were away. Before, this person was like a sheikh and he had lots of people working for him.

It normally took two days to get to the place where we would dive – the places were Al Raila, Umm Al Sheif, Abu Al Bekhoush and Abu Kharis. There were boats there from Dubai, Abu Dhabi, Sharjah, Umm Al Qaiwain and Ras Al Khaimah.

It was not very comfortable on board the boat and it was very tough work. We would dive from morning to evening. Very early in the morning was the call to prayer and everybody

had to get up and get ready for the day. Before we prayed we would use sea water to clean ourselves. We would then dive for three hours, after which the captain would tell us to come up. We would eat a few dates and drink some coffee, but not much more than that.

Each diver had a *saib* up on the boat, who pulled him up by a rope. The *saib* wouldn't sit, instead he was always standing because he had to be ready to pull up the diver when he felt the tug on the rope. We had a *fatam* on our noses to keep the water from going in, weights on our feet to take us down and a *diyyin*, like a bucket, around our necks to collect the shells. We would stay under the water for several minutes. Some people would stay more, some less, but of course if you stayed down longer you would get more shells.

First I was a *saib*, then I was a diver. When people were young they would come on the dive to learn as helpers and *saibs* and then slowly, slowly they became divers. I was a good diver, by God. The *nokhada* used to say I was good.

Sometimes we went down eight, nine, ten metres, sometimes more – it depended on the different depths of the places we dived. There was one place, at the island at Abu Al Bekhoush, that was very deep. It was about 15 metres down. We did so many dives each day – I don't know how many. We would only come up on the boat for *Dhuhr* and *Asr* prayers. We stayed at the surface for just three or four minutes. We knew we had to go down again. Some of the *nokhadas* would beat the people if they didn't go down because the captains had spent a lot of money going diving and they had to bring pearls back. The divers couldn't do anything – they had debts with the captains. They never said no. They had to dive.

If a man was beaten at sea he could do nothing there, but after, when we were back in Dubai he could go to see Sheikh Hasher bin Maktoum. He was the judge. Once, a man was beaten at sea and he went to the judge. The Sheikh told him to bring people who saw this happen – witnesses. They came. After that the judge had the *nokhada* brought and he was beaten by two men. Thank God, nothing like this happened on our boat.

There was not much food to be eaten on board. We had very light meals and the only proper meal was in the evening. We ate mostly rice and fish and dates. One time, the *imam* on our boat took one of the fish for dinner from the fire and put it with his things. He didn't know there was a hot ember still sticking to the fish. We were making our prayers and then suddenly we saw smoke rising on the other side of the boat. That's when we found the *imam* had the fish there.

To drink there was water and a little coffee. There was a special cup put on the water tank which was very small. It was not enough for one person, but you had to take only one cup. The captain was always watching you so you didn't take more than that. Each one of us could drink only what the captain would allow so we felt thirsty for the whole day.

'Each one of us could drink only what the captain would allow so we felt thirsty for the whole day.'

We were in the sea all day but we couldn't have a shower so our skin became very rough. We put *qarat* on it to try to make it better before we went to sleep.

We never dived during Ramadan. It was not allowed.

There was a lot of competition between the divers and between the captains. They would say I brought this pearl, I brought that one. Everybody knew if a good pearl had been found. We made piles of shells on the deck and in the evening we would see who had brought the most. The one who brought the most, the captain liked him a lot. The *nokhada* would tell us to stop when the boat was full of shells. We would open some shells in the afternoon and others the next morning. Once the shells were opened, they were thrown back in the water.

Some people tried to steal pearls, but they were caught. After that the *nokhada* put two people watching the others all the time. No-one sang or spoke when we were opening the pearls. It was very serious. The captain would have a small wooden box to keep the pearls inside. It was always with him and he would never leave it – he would sleep on that box. Maybe if you found one pearl, a good one, a *hasbah* they could get 1,500 rupees for it. The best one I ever got, they sold it for around 1,000 rupees.

When it was a good year we would get 30, 35 or 40 rupees for three months work. The maximum was 50 or 60 – nobody reached 100 rupees. The money from the pearls would be shared – after the costs of the boat, getting it ready, the food and money for the owner, the rest would be divided up depending on how many divers and *saibs* there were. The divers got more money than the *saibs*.

'As I went to sleep I could hear the live shells underneath me.'

Sometimes, if a diver was very good, he would get maybe 10 rupees extra when the diving finished. This was a lot of money then. It was like a bonus, but I never got this.

After praying in the evening we would do nothing. The captain said everyone must sleep. Some people said their *Maghrib* and *Isha* prayers together so they could sleep earlier. Mostly we slept on top of the shells as there was no other space on the deck. We put out a mat made from date palm leaves. Each person had one each. As I went to sleep I could hear the live shells underneath me.

We didn't come back to Dubai during the diving. If there was bad weather or strong winds we would go to an island for one or two days for shelter and then go diving again.

I was a *naham*, a singer, on the boat. There were two people who sang onboard our boat. When we moved from one place to another and there wasn't any wind to use the sails, we'd have to use the oars. This is when we sang. The singing was to make us stronger and give ourselves more power. We would move three or four times each day. The *nokhada* would say, "Everybody up, let's go." There wasn't a particular time of day that we moved, just when we needed to, to dive for more pearls.

Everybody came back home together. We had to follow the *sirdal* who was Juma Abdullah Al Amlah. He decided when it was the end of diving. He was very experienced – he was the captain of a boat, but he was very well known by the captains of the other boats. Towards the end of diving, for ten days everybody would watch this man, this *sirdal*, to see what he was doing, where he was going, when he would put up the flag which meant it was the end of the diving season. When the red and white flag of Dubai went up it meant we could go home. We were very happy. When we were going home it was like Eid – even better than Eid. We would shave and get ourselves ready. There was a feeling of celebration on board. All night everybody would laugh, dance, clap and enjoy the journey. When we reached land, we would lift up our own boat, clean it and then everybody would go home.

Sometimes I think back to when we were under the sea – there was fear, but what could we do? When we were under the water we could see jellyfish or a shark coming near, but we wanted to eat. We were diving for money, for food – to live. It was life.

Bilal lives by the sea in Jumeirah. He visits the Fishermen's Majlis in Umm Sequim each day to be with his friends and to reminisce.

CHAPTER 3

The Bedouin

OBAID HUMAID ABID AL MUHAIRI
& FATIMA SALIM EID AL MANSOURI

TRANSLATED BY THEIR SON AND DAUGHTER-IN-LAW, SAIF OBAID AL MUHAIRI AND LATIFA SAEED AL MANSOURI

I was born in 1933 in Jumeirah. I have two brothers, no sisters. Life then was fine here – better than in other countries. The local men went diving and fishing and they brought things like clothes from India. The Creek was used for this, to bring things by boat. My father was the *nokhada* of a diving boat in the summer – he had 40 people with him. Then in the winter he was fishing and he was the boss. He had fishermen to catch the fish and he would sell them.

In Jumeirah, our family's house was near the beach, opposite where my house is now. In the winter it was a *khaimah* made from date palm leaves and in summer it was an *areesh* house. I remember fishing and playing on the beach with my father. I didn't go to school. From when I was eight or ten I would go with my mother's brothers, Mubarak and Saif, to the desert with the camels and goats. We had eight camels, some for carrying wood and others for milk. I lived in the desert with them. My uncles wanted to teach me everything they knew and step by step I learnt, so my uncles trusted me. I learnt how to teach camels but it wasn't easy – camels, like horses, don't know how to behave with Man.

My uncles showed me how to cut the wood in the desert, what size it should be, how to put it on the camel and where to sell this wood. I sold it to whoever needed wood when I saw them or I took it to the market in Shindagha. It was only around two Indian rupees for a whole load of wood – it was cheap, but it was the only thing we had to sell. The best wood was *ghaff* or *samar*, but we didn't have samar here – that was in Ras Al Khaimah.

Throughout the year we would move about. Usually we went towards Abu Dhabi, but in the days of war between Abu Dhabi and Dubai we went to Khawaneej. Bedouin would go wherever there was water. We would pack everything – tent and food – onto the camel and we would go.

In the summer we went from Jumeirah to Al Ain and it would take five days by camel. There would be maybe five or ten people in the group. We would leave at four in the afternoon and go to Towi Rasheed near Nad Al Sheba. We slept there in the desert under the sky, then at four in the morning we would wake up and travel until ten. Then it was very hot for us and the camels – we would stop to rest until four and walk again until the evening when we slept. We knew the places which had water and we knew we had to keep walking until we got to them.

'We knew the places which had water and we knew we had to keep walking until we got to them.'

When I was around 17 or 18 I met Mubarak bin London (1) a few times at Nad Al Sheba. He slept outside my tent, behind where I was staying. You wouldn't know he was not an Arab – he wore a *khizam*, he had a camel and carried a gun sticking up over his shoulder like the Arabs. He was a tall man and he wore a red *kandoura*. He spoke Arabic very well and he would do whatever the Arab people did – he would eat the same food, like hare with rice.

At special times we had camel races because the families like Al Muhairi or Al Mansouri always said they had the best camel. So they raced to see who really had the best – just like the ruling families, Al Nahyan in Abu Dhabi and Al Maktoum in Dubai. One time in the year there was a big race between the sheikhs of Abu Dhabi and Dubai. It started where there is a police station now at Saih Sheyb and the finish was behind Jebel Ali. There were about 25 or 30 camels racing. They were different ages, but they were all fit. It was about 25 kilometres or more across the desert there and flat with no dunes.

There was another race from Jumeirah to Shindagha. It was a smaller race, but many people came to see it. People put saffron on the head of the camel which won – it had a very nice smell and it was like a gift for the camel. Everywhere the camel went for a week the people could smell it.

We would have camel races at weddings and sometimes I raced myself. I won a race riding a female camel – they were the best racers. The camel was a red colour and her name was Araana. I was 25 years old or more. It was normal for us to ride camels – that's how we went everywhere. We didn't think it was dangerous.

I was born at Nad Al Sheba in the desert at a special place we call Towi Rasheed. My grandfather dug the well there and we would stay in that place in summer. Before, when babies were born in the desert, the women would bring a piece of wood and bang it into the sand. They would hold on to this wood and pull on it when they were having the baby.

In winter we lived in a *bayt al shaar* made of sheep hair. It was very small. In the winter we moved around inside the desert. I would look after the goats and go walking with them. Once, when I was about five I went out with our goats in the afternoon and it became dark so I couldn't find my way home. My father had a camel and came looking for me. He saw the footprints of all the goats and found me.

After *Maghrib* prayers we would bring wood to make a fire and we would drink milk. We would sit in the evening listening to stories and talking about what we had done and what we would do the next day.

Later, I lived in Jumeirah in a house made from date palm branches. My mother had died when I was two years old so my father looked after me, my two brothers and my sister. There wasn't much work at that time. My father would go to the beach to catch fish or he would cut wood in the desert and sell it at the market in Dubai. We had two camels as transport and for carrying the wood my father cut, but we didn't have them for milk. Our neighbour would send camel milk to us.

When we were young we ate rice with oil and yoghurt and the bread my father made. When I was older I did the cooking. We didn't have gas, only wood to make a fire.

I also got the food ready for our camels. The camels ate dates – cheap dates from Iran that were too hard for people to eat. I put them in water for a long time and then when they were soft I would mash them. The camels would also graze on their own, but our camels knew that every day there was food for them at our house. My father would tell my brother to make the food for the camels, but he wanted to play with his friends and would say to me, "Fatima, you make it. If you don't I will beat you!"

When I was seven, I went for one year to a woman who taught us The Koran at a house in Jumeirah. My father paid a little money. Every morning the teacher would read the words first and then all the children would read together.

'I was thirteen when I got married. I didn't know what it meant to be married except that I could put on kohl and henna.'

My father got a job as a security guard at the British Bank of the Middle East and after that he got married again. It was one of the best days of my life – I was around nine years old. My mother, Latifa, had died before I could remember her and I felt I was alone. When my father remarried I had a mother again.

There were some date palms in Jumeirah, but in the old times, as soon as the dates came, people would eat them straight away, for freshness. Each house would have three, four or five date palms. Later they would buy dates from Iran and Iraq – from Basra. At that time people didn't have big farms – in Dubai the people didn't have anything.

I was thirteen when I got married. I don't have any papers, but it was around the time of *Ittihad*. I didn't know what it meant to be married except that I could put on kohl and henna. The wedding was for two days near my father's house. There was singing and dancing – we had the *ayyala*. Lots of people came, but I don't know how many because I stayed in the house. Nobody saw me. I wore a green *kandoura* with red decorations and a *burqa*, *shayla* and *abaya* covering my face. I had a gold necklace and special jewellery on my hands. My husband bought this for me. My dowry was 10,000 Qatar and Dubai riyals plus the food for the party, my gold and food for the store at my father's house – 50 kilos of rice and sugar and tea. Also there were some clothes to be given as gifts to the neighbours.

I had never met my husband before. I was the second wife for him, but I was small so I didn't think about that. My father told my husband, "If you want my daughter, after marriage she will stay with me in my house." I stayed there for about six years and then we had a small house close to my father's home. When I saw Obaid for the first time I was afraid. I was young and he was older, but after that it was alright – I loved him.

Obaid and Fatima live surrounded by their extended family on the Beach Road in Jumeirah.

Obaid visits the camels at his farm near the Emirates Road every day.

1. Arabic name for Sir Wilfred Thesiger, the British explorer and author of 'Arabian Sands' who crossed the Empty Quarter in the 1940s.

CHAPTER 4

Sheikh Mohammed Bin Rashid with Hamed Bin Sougat

The Loyal Companion

HAMAD BIN AHMED BIN HAMAD BIN SOUGAT

TRANSLATED BY HIS SON, ABDULLA BIN HAMAD BIN SOUGAT

I was born in Al Ras in Deira, west of the house of Sheikh Butti bin Suhail, the former ruler of Dubai. (1) I don't remember which year I was born, but it was around 1930.

My father went to Al Hasa, which is in Saudi Arabia now. He studied the religion of Islam – an intensive programme we call *Al Shariah*. Then he was sent back to Dubai where he became a person to whom people would ask questions about religion. He was more of a teacher than a normal person. He used to be an *imam* for the royal family's mosques here in Dubai. Those mosques used to pay the *imams* money and that was his salary.

I studied at Al Ahmadiya School. After I left school, I accompanied Sheikh Rashid all my life until he passed away. I was his private companion. I was with him in Dubai as well as anywhere he went outside the country. Sheikh Rashid was a very intelligent man – someone who looked to the future rather than just the present. He was a very impressive person. Even back then he wanted Dubai to be the number one city. He used to maintain good relations with outside and the neighbouring countries. Most of the things he foresaw back then, they actually came true.

People in the *majlis* did not believe such development was going to take place, but Sheikh Rashid, he believed it. He started with the digging of The Creek. That was his main concern. Dubai was a dock where a lot of ships came from the surrounding areas for trade. Then Sheikh Rashid established Dubai Municipality of which I was a founding board member. He introduced electricity to Dubai and he organised the city.

I was in the *majlis* the night it became known how much money was needed for the dredging of The Creek. (2) People knew it was a lot of money, but most of the people agreed with the decision that was taken and the money that was being spent. Back then Sheikh Rashid

took loans from the bank and from some neighbouring countries as well. After the deepening of The Creek he started selling some of the plots that were around the water and paid back the banks and the other countries. When this development started a lot of people were happy. They knew that Sheikh Rashid's decision was going to pay dividends to the government and to the society.

Sheikh Rashid started his days early in the morning. He would take a look around the city until eight o'clock. Then he returned home, had breakfast, after which he went to his office, where the Ruler's Court is, until one o'clock. Then he went back home, he rested for a while and came back out at four o'clock. He got in his car and he drove around the city. Then he went to his majlis in Jumeirah until eight or nine o'clock. From there he went back to Zabeel where he stayed in his house, in his majlis, until 12 midnight.

In the majlis there were a lot of people, not less than 60 or 70 people at any one time. His private companions were around 20 or 25 in number.

Sheikh Rashid was a humble man. He did not have complications about who was going to see him and who he would speak to. He had open offices and an open *majlis*. Anybody could come in and start a conversation with Sheikh Rashid – it was not like they had to stand in a queue or even make an appointment. Sheikh Rashid acted as a normal person.

He did not like to be segregated in any *majlis*. He didn't feel he had to act differently because he was the ruler of the city. When we used to go camping, for a picnic or on a falconry trip, Sheikh Rashid would sit with us on the sand and put his arm around the shoulder of the person he was next to. He was very down-to-earth.

Sheikh Rashid used to throw in a subject to everyone in the *majlis*. He would let them discuss it in front of him. He would not participate in it – he just had to hear what was said. He used to create the subject for them and let them fight over it. People would throw in ideas, give opinions and suggestions and he would take the conclusion. He would just keep it to himself. Sheikh Rashid was not a person who would sit alone by himself and start thinking. Instead he always wanted people around him and he wanted to take decisions with people, not alone.

Sheikh Rashid was a patient person. He didn't like to show his nerves with people, nor to take action at that moment and be harsh. He was very straightforward. There is a story of a gentlemen who was a friend of Sheikh Rashid. He came and asked Sheikh Rashid for something. He repeated his question many times. Well, Sheikh Rashid, he got tired of it, and he said, "You know, you don't even know how to ask people for what you want." The man said, "Well, this is the way I ask. Do you want me to bring a musician to play the violin for you while I ask you something?" Sheikh Rashid laughed a lot.

Sheikh Rashid had three phrases for anyone who had ideas and suggestions; either, "Go ahead and good luck with it," or, "Let me have two days to think about it," or, "Just forget it". Any ideas that would benefit Dubai, Sheikh Rashid would tell people to

'After I left school, I accompanied Sheikh Rashid all my life until he passed away. I was his private companion.'

In 1968, on the way back from a morning visit to Sheikh Zayed's farm at Khawaneej with Sheikh Rashid, I suggested to him that I wanted to build my house in the area we were passing through and to start developing that area. I felt the city was congested so I wanted to move out. Sheikh Rashid agreed to it and said he would provide a small restaurant and a petrol station in what became Rashidiya. There were no buildings at that time – it was just desert with camels, cattle, sheep and goats. Sheikh Rashid gave permission so I gave out the plots and signed the plans and they were then submitted to The Municipality. In that way Rashidiya developed as its own city.

go ahead with and then he would encourage them as well. He would also check that they were following their plans through – if they didn't he would withdraw his support.

We used to go camp in the area where Jebel Ali Port is now. We would go for about two weeks with tents and some *areesh* around the campfire where we used to sit at night. There were around 100 to 150 people at night who would have dinner and then go back to the city. Only Sheikh Rashid's special companions would stay there. We would sleep over, then come to Dubai each morning and act normally. When we went camping, Sheikh Rashid would often be drawing lines in the sand with a stick and making plans, but no one really knew what

'We used to fight each other, then we became one union.'

he was thinking. When he revealed the news about Jebel Ali Port people in the town were very surprised, but he had been planning it for some time.

Some people were nervous about federation, some people were very happy, but knowledgeable people knew that the union, the federation of the UAE, was going to be more of an advantage than a disadvantage. Sheikh Rashid was very anxious at this time as he and Sheikh Zayed were the base of the union. We thought it was a good thing for us because instead of being small states now we became a single country. We used to fight each other, then we became one union. Some of the rulers of the emirates were nervous about it, but things were clarified to them and people were happy.

When I think of Sheikh Rashid now I think of him as being a hero. Whenever I think of him I picture that hero. But these things are all just memories and they will never come back

Hamad lives in Rashidiya where his family owns the Bin Sougat Centre shopping mall.

1. 1906-1912.
2. £600,000, 'Father of Dubai' Wilson, 1999, p. 81.

The Pearl Merchant

MOHAMED ABDUL RAZZAQ ABDUL RAHIM AL BASTAKI

I was born on January 5th 1916 at the Bastaki family house in Bastakia. (1)
My family came from Bastak, a town in southern Iran, close to Dubai.
Then we came to stay in the Bastakia area here. It was our home.

Sheikh Maktoum, Sheikh Saeed's father (2) wanted us to come to Dubai. We were coming and going for 20 or 30 years, but around 1900 we settled because Sheikh Maktoum told us to come and stay here. He said people would shift from the area we called Bastakia to Deira and leave this area for all of us. "You bring your family," he told my father.

My father was Abdul Razzaq Abdul Rahim. He was a very good man, well-known here, in Kuwait and in Bahrain because he was just and decent. People in Dubai – all the Arabs and the Bastakis – they knew my father. He always told me to tell the truth. He was respected – Sheikh Saeed respected him a lot.

I remember swimming when I was young. There was nothing else at that time – Bastakia was the border of Dubai town so it was either sea or desert on each side. Our house was just by The Creek. I was a great swimmer so they called me 'The Fish'.

I went to school in Deira, to Al Ahmadiya School. Sheikh Rashid went to this school too, but he finished one or two years before me. There were four classes. I knew how to read a book before I went to school. We did Arabic, Religion of course, and Maths. There was some 'a b c d' – a little English. There were about 150 children and 40 children per class, all of them locals. The teachers were from Iraq, from Zubair. They were kind, but they were very strict. Everyday pupils received lashings.

We finished school about one o'clock or half past one, but no later. We came home by *abra* across The Creek. At that time there were about five, six, seven *abras* only. The people who rowed the *abras* were local people from Dubai. My father gave me money for the *abra*, but one day I lost the money. What could I do? I had to swim. I tied everything in my *wezar* and '*Yalla*'! I remember I jumped in the water with my friend, Bu Jaber and we swam. The water was with us. We made it to Sheikh Saeed's House in Shindagha. From there I walked to Bastakia and got dry. I never told my father I got wet that day.

My family was dealing in pearls – we were *tawwash*. We bought the pearls from the captain of the ship, the *nokhada*, here in Dubai and we took them to Bombay. People would bring the pearls to the *majlis* in our house in Bastakia.

'I started working when I was 12 years old and I knew pearls by that age.'

I started working when I was 12 years old and I knew pearls by that age – I learned about them from my father. My nickname was 'Jowhari' – the person who knows about gems. They called me Mohamed Jowhari. My father would give the pearls to me for weighing because I am honest. Sometimes when I was weighing them it was to the other person's benefit so people wanted me to weigh for them. I was around 15 – it was before I was married – when I became a judge of pearls. Some people disagreed over the prices, so Sheikh Rashid said, "Go to him and he'll be the judge." All the experts were in their 20's and 30's, but I knew more than the others. My father had taught me.

All kinds of pearls came from the sea, even dust, but when people brought them to me I separated them into different types with a sieve which had seven different size meshes. The *jiwan* (3) was the best grade, the second grade was *yakka* (it means ace) then *golwa*, *badlah*, *khashar*, *nawaem* and *bouka*. The size, colour and shape were all important when deciding how good a pearl was. The best coloured pearls were in our sea – the Dubai sea. Pearls were coming from Kuwait, from Bahrain, from Qatar, but ours were the best – they were a kind of rose colour.

Once a year, in July or August, we went to Bombay, which took ten days. We went on the British India Steam Navigation company ships – the 'Bandra' and 'Barpeta' were two of them. We were in first class, in the cabin. We took thousands of rupees worth of pearls with us. I didn't worry about being robbed – nobody knew what I had. We sold the pearls in Bombay and the Indians would make necklaces to send to Paris and then from Paris they were sent to America.

I brought the first football to Dubai in 1928 – when I was 12. From Bahrain I was hearing all about football so when I went to Bombay with my father to sell pearls I said, "Baba, I want this – they call it a football." He bought one for five rupees. I was playing alone in Bastakia when Khalifa bin Saeed, Sheikh Rashid's brother came along and asked, "What is this? *Gubbat Shaitan*! – Devil's ball!" He laughed and kicked it into The Creek. Another time the ball got punctured by a thorny tree – we had to wait six months before going to Bombay again. That time we bought two inside parts – one spare.

We played near where the British Embassy is now. We didn't know how to play and just tried to get goals ourselves. Then a man, Poore Foulad, came from Bahrain and told us there were rules, positions and 11-a-side. Later, Bastakia played Shindagha and Deira played Dubai. It was very competitive – at times people wouldn't talk for a month after a game.

In the 1930s when we were going to Bombay the market for pearls was very low. I remember once we had 80,000 rupees worth of pearls with us and the people said they couldn't buy all of them. I divided the total number into four groups. It was very complicated to divide the pearls to make them the most saleable and expensive, but I did it and took them to the Jowhari Bazaar. The buyer couldn't tell the difference between the four groups of pearls. We sold them all for the highest price. After that I was sick for a month – it was very difficult and complicated work. (4)

Mohamed lives in Jumeirah with his wife, Noora.

Their house is often full of the sounds of their children and grandchildren.

1. Now 'Bastakia Nights' restaurant.
2. Sheikh Maktoum bin Hasher, Ruler of Dubai 1894-1906.
3. A derivative of G-One or Grade One.
4. The unit for weighing pearls and valuing them was the *chow*. The merchants used special handbooks with columns of tables to decide on their value and how best to divide a group of pearls to get the best price.

The Bastakis of Bastakia

From left to right

RUQAIYA, NABIL, MOHAMAD, YOUSEF, FARIDA AND EESA

Ruqaiya I was born 10th February 1942 in Bastakia.   My family had a pearl business with India. Our relatives all lived in Al Bastakia. There was no electricity so each evening in every house we would clean the lanterns and light them up for the night. There were windtowers on most houses and even if there was a little breeze from any side, it would be drawn down and you would feel it. We would call it God's breeze. There weren't many rooms in the house, but they were big – each was for a husband, wife and their children together. The men would sit in the *majlis* by the main entrance and there was a separate room just for books. (1) Men from outside the family would come there in the evenings and on Fridays.

In the winter it would get very cold so we lived downstairs. It would rain heavily and water would collect in the compound – we could paddle in the courtyard. In summer we would move upstairs onto the terrace. There were patterned screens built into the house so the breeze from The Creek would blow through.

From up there we could see The Creek – it was wider than now and not so deep. The dhows were anchored in the middle because it was shallow on the edge. When we were young we would row out in our little tin boat and climb up to play on them.

Every morning when the men went to work, our close relatives would gather at our house because my grandmother was the eldest lady. There would be about eight to ten women doing stitching and embroidery, chatting and drinking tea or coffee. When the *Dhuhr* call to prayer came and it was time for the men to come home, the ladies would leave. In the afternoon, after *Asr* prayers, the men went back to work and the ladies returned to our house. News was spread

in this way and gossip was part of the fun. The women would say, "This one had a baby, this one's husband did that and that one's wife did that." There was all sorts of gossip and teasing.

At night, in the middle of each month when the moon was bright, (2) the ladies would go to The Creek. We would splash about, but we didn't know how to swim. We kept our dresses on and the men knew it was ladies' night so they didn't dare come near!

The Creek was the heart of the city because there were only a few areas – Shindagha, Bastakia and in between there was another place where some Bahrainis lived. Different communities had different places. We didn't go to the other side of The Creek very often – I only remember going once or twice to Deira.

When I was born there was no hospital and no doctors so my mother had me in the house. There were two or three midwives my family knew who came to help at births. The men would go out of the house. A lot of babies died at birth – I was the only one who survived among my mother's children. I had an elder brother, Abdullah, who died when he was about six months old. I think he had pneumonia. I was two years old when my mother had a girl who died after two weeks and within a month of her delivery my mother also died. Many women died at childbirth. At first my grandmother looked after me and later my mother's sister took care of me. She then married my father.

My age group of girls here was not educated and I think I was the only one to go to India to study. I didn't know at the time what a great opportunity it was, but later I was very grateful to my father. When I got there, people didn't know where Dubai was – it wasn't on the map. At that time the only thing that was known was Sharjah so I told them it was near there.

Yousef I was born 29th March 1952, Eesa on the 25th December 1955 and Nabil 5th August 1965. I remember when Eesa was born. There was an American hospital in Sharjah and he was born in the car on the way there. It was Christmas Day – that's why he's called Eesa. (3)

Eesa I am the middle one of nine children. My mother had been trying to delay the birth because it was her mother's cousin's wedding and she wanted to go to the party. The family eventually had to carry her from Dubai to Deira on the abra and there was a car on Deira side. That became the car I was born in!

Yousef The weddings took place for seven nights in a row so we went there and slept. I was young so I used to go with the ladies. I was too young to notice if they were glamorous women – I only started looking when I was ten! I just enjoyed the dancing and singing.

Eesa The men had their own fun with musicians singing and dancing.

'I was too young to notice if they were glamorous women.'

Yousef In front of our house there was an open space and sometimes people would come to dance, even in the late 1960s it continued. They'd come and make a circle, going forwards and back with their sticks and with a *habban* – an instrument made from the skin of a goat.

Ruqaiya I remember my uncle's wedding. In those days the weddings were in the bride's house. The couples used to be relatives, like cousins, so this wedding was in my aunt's house – very nearby. Marriage then was like an exchange – their girl came to our house and our girl went to their house. The weddings would be for six or seven days and the brides didn't wear white, but had different colours on each day; red one day, then green, purple, orange – all with golden embroidery. They had heavy gold ornaments on their head like a cap with gold coins all joined

together, three necklaces, thick bangles, big earrings and nose rings. The gold was within the family passed down from previous generations. Women would also borrow jewellery from relatives. There was a big metal box in the house with a key where our jewellery was kept.

Everybody in the area was invited to the wedding. Around a week before Bastakia weddings, certain ladies, called *zangardoun*, who knew all the houses, would go door-to-door with cardamom seeds either in a bowl or on coloured threads and this was the invitation to the wedding.

During the celebrations people would come day or night for breakfast, lunch or dinner. All the food came from the groom's family; it was cooked at their home and brought to the bride's house. The groom would give gold and clothes and pay for the wedding food. The ladies' party was in the courtyard, a drum was played and the women would hold square silk cloths, like handkerchiefs, with coloured beads on them and dance and sing. There's a Persian name for it – *dastmolbozi*. The songs were Bastaki songs from Bastak.

Back then we didn't know what a honeymoon was – on the wedding night and for a week or two the couple stayed at the bride's house. Her family made sure she got used to her husband in her own mother's house. Their room would be decorated with coloured glass balls, silk materials and embroidery. Then the bride would be invited to the groom's house for another big party and she'd stay after that.

Back then the bride and the groom wouldn't have seen each other before the wedding. From the time a girl became mature she didn't really move out of her house even within Bastakia. In front of first cousins and beyond the girls would cover their faces. Before marriage the girls weren't allowed to wear make up, gold or flashy dresses, so they wanted to get married early – it was normal at 14 or 15. It was to do with dressing up – nothing to do with the boys! If the women wanted to choose anyone for their sons this was done at weddings. The unmarried girls could only go to the celebrations at night and they would sit shyly in one room and hide their faces when a married lady came in, although really they liked the idea they might be chosen. They all wanted to get married and become 'free' as we called it.

Yousef I went to the *muttawa* school when I was four or five which was two houses down from our house. Sheikh Abdul Rahim was a very, very strict person and he used to beat the children who didn't do their work. He would either have a bigger boy carry you on his back and he walloped you from behind or he strung you up and beat the soles of your feet. It was very effective! I never got beaten and I finished The Koran very quickly. That was how I learned to read and write.

Eesa   We played many games – soccer, marbles, *mistaa* – which is like cricket and baseball. Another one was *gilili matooaa*. There was a stick for a bat and a smaller stick with sharp ends. The further you hit it the more points you got. If you missed it three times you were out. The ladies used to play football in the courtyard of the house. In the summer, we would swim daily in the morning, then go back for lunch, then swim again. Sometimes we swam to Sheikha Mariam's palace by the Maktoum Bridge because they had some sweet fruits called *louz*.

Yousef   An Indian man had a small tea shop on the Deira side and my cousin and I used to go for tea and then run away without paying. We'd jump into The Creek and swim back. Other times cousins had tubes and would sit on them to get taken by the current. I had to swim out to get them because I was the eldest.

Nabil   Once, when I was about five I was walking on the shore past the Maktoum Bridge and there was a deep hole because of the boats which anchored there. I fell in; I was going up and down and I couldn't breathe. Someone screamed, "Nabil is drowning!" When Yousef saved me I thought a shark had come!

Farida   I've been told I was born in Bastakia on 5th August 1948 at home. Most of the houses were built close together with small lanes and it was like a maze – ideal for playing hide-and-seek.

I was a chubby baby so my Dad would show me off to Sheikh Rashid – they were great friends. Sheikh Rashid would take me in his arms and bounce me up and down. We looked forward to my Dad coming back from his hunting trips with Sheikh Rashid as he would bring big houbara birds and gazelles. Biryani was made using the houbara and we'd munch on dried gazelle meat which was delicious. The water that came by donkey was kept in jars – the sort you imagine Ali Baba would hide in. They were made of ceramic and as the water evaporated the surface of the jar stayed damp and cool. Any residue and even worms settled at the bottom.

After the pearling had mostly finished, the family switched to the wholesale business. My dad decided to import water filters so we were the first ones to have a filter and therefore purified water. I made a dolls' house on the sand in our courtyard out of the huge box that the water filters came in. One of the Sheikh's relatives, a little girl, took a fancy to it so my dad presented it to them.

We had thick pyramids of sugar in the house. We would break off a piece and put it in a glass with some lemon juice and cool water. This was before we had ice. I remember the first fridge with kerosene flames underneath to cool the inside. We were lucky to have a lot of things first when others had them only later.

We couldn't go far from Bastakia – if we went to Shindagha it was like going to another country because you had to go across the desert.

I remember a fire when I was around eight. There were some houses made out of barasti nearby and a fire started in one. Our whole house caught alight and I had to take my three little brothers out of the house to walk to my Dad's office which was past Shindagha. Eesa was so small I had to carry him. When I got there the adults could see the black smoke for themselves. Our house survived, but the houses of the poor people in the barastis were totally destroyed and of course the Sheikh helped them with blankets and so on.

After *maktab* I went to school in Bombay. My grandfather, Abdul Razzaq, was a big name there – people would salute him and call him 'Arab Saheb'. I remember he would still lay out pearls on red velvet with lots of different sieves to separate them from big to medium, medium to small. People came to buy directly from him. My grandfather was very honest and would never do anything that wasn't legal anywhere. He thought the gold smuggling was wrong – he'd see it everywhere but he wouldn't do it – he felt he had enough business anyway. He passed away still leading the business.

Yousef We had a special Bastaki language. It's a mixture of Persian and Arabic. Eighty percent or so is Arabic, but the accent is more Persian and it's a dialect that started in the south of Iran. In those days we spoke Bastaki at home. We still do with our father.

Eesa We had two groups that defended Bastakia, one at each end. The head of one was my late cousin, Faisal and the other was Salim Ismail. They weren't gangs, but they protected the girls from those outside Bastakia. It was necessary because some youths would come to flirt – it was to protect the honour of the girls.

Yousef The locusts used to come in their thousands, usually in the autumn from Africa. They looked like clouds filling the sky and they would strip the trees of leaves. They'd settle on The Creek or on the land and we used to catch them in sacks and cook them. We'd eat the whole locust except the wings and I remember they were crunchy. One year the British sprayed them and told us not to eat them.

Eesa In 1975, towards the end of school I was teaching my friends different subjects to pass the exams. We would drive to the airport because it had very bright lights so it was a good place to study. (4)

Yousef I went to school in Bombay and lived there with our grandparents. Schools were much better there. I didn't come back for ten years, until 1969. You wouldn't believe the happy feelings I had about coming home. Back then the big ships anchored a few kilometres off the coast of Dubai and the immigration people boarded at sea. Small boats would then bring the passengers to the city. As soon as I saw Dubai Creek I just wanted to jump in.

All nine Bastaki children are graduates in subjects as varied as Medicine, Engineering, Electronics and Philosophy and Islamic Studies. All of the boys have PhDs and Ruqaiya holds a Masters – testament they say to their father's belief in education. Ruqaiya, Yousef, Eesa and Nabil live in Dubai. Farida lives in Australia.

1. Believed to be the first 'library' in Dubai.
2. Islamic months are dictated by the sighting of the new moon so the full moon would always be in the middle of the month.
3. Translation of Jesus.
4. See Chapter 17, 'The Aviator'.

CHAPTER 7

The Nokhada

SAIF AHMED AL GHURAIR

TRANSLATED BY HIS SON, RASHID AL GHURAIR

I was born at home in Deira, on the shores of The Creek – opposite Shindagha. It was 1924. I know this because there was a learned man – Hamad Bin Sougat's father (1) – who wrote it down. Our house is still there and they've changed it into small shops. It was a nice house made of stone and *jus* – not cement, not mud, but in between – a white or cream colour. It had 16 or 17 people living in it including family and servants.

My grandfather, Majid, was a *tajir*. He owned four or five ships that were used for pearl diving, but he didn't go pearling himself. He was a philanthropist and would take care of sick people. I remember when there was plague and my grandfather was kind and would help people. When my grandfather was alive, my father would help him with his work. He was the *nokhada* of a *sanbouk*. Later, I worked with my father and went pearl diving and on trade missions on his behalf. In my grandfather's time, it was the height of the pearl diving period and everybody was wealthy and didn't need to do other work. However in my father's time pearl diving declined because of the artificial pearls coming from Japan, but we still continued because we didn't have anything else.

I went on the dive with my father when I was young, but when I was a teenager I went alone as the *nokhada*. It was extremely hard. Sometimes we would find fish to eat, but if we didn't we would eat only dates and rice at the end of the day. We would spend four months at sea without coming back. I had good people with me – people I could rely on and who my father could trust. I used to take care of the pearls and keep them with me.

When the shells were being opened, I would have four people – two on either side – to make sure no-one took any pearls. The people opening would sit in a row and the other people would sit opposite them and make sure none were taken. It did happen, but not as often as on other boats and if we were lucky we would catch them. The pearls were kept in a small wooden box. I would put the box inside a compartment in the boat, close the lid and sleep on top.

'The next day the sailors were so scared that when they made their lunch, they didn't eat it!'

We used to sell our pearls in Dubai – to local people and also Indian agents who would take them to India. The crew would take a percentage of the gathering from the sea, so if a *dana* was found they would be very happy. The owner of the boat took one fifth. The cost of food, water and repairs would be deducted and then there would be a division among the crew. The divers got perhaps double what the *saibs* working on the boat would have got and the *nokhada* got the same as the divers, not more. It depended on the owner – sometimes he would give the *nokhada* a reward.

By the time I went diving in the 1930s the catch was only worth around 7,000 Indian rupees altogether, but in the time of my grandfather it would have been worth much more – around 100,000. I would get paid the same as the divers but with a bonus from the owner – my father. The money used to go back into the family.

In World War Two we fixed the pearling boats and started trading – to Africa, India and Iran. We also used some supply boats that had previously brought water and food to the divers – they were smaller and riskier to travel in. We would take dates from Iraq to Africa and from India we would bring back textiles and logs of teak for boat building.

At the time of the war the area was under British protection so the British were helpful to this region – they would bring rations of tea, sugar, rice and so on because there were no supplies. The people here were so poor they were selling their rations and then some people would buy them and take them to Iran to make a better profit. Many people made money trading like that.

Later, we started taking dates to India. At first we would buy the imported dates from here to take and later we went to Basra in Iraq to buy them directly.

Once, we were in Mombasa, which was then still under British rule, and we bought ammunition for our rifles. There were African soldiers under the British command who would sell their bullets. One man asked me if I wanted to buy 40 boxes of ammunition. Each box had around 1,000 bullets and they were very cheap because they were stolen from the British. I agreed to buy them and in the middle of the night they brought the ammunition to the boat. My crew had thought he would bring a box or two, but when he came with 40 boxes they refused to take them. I told him to put them in the hold while we talked about it.

The next day the sailors were so scared that when they made their lunch, they didn't eat it! They were worried about what would happen if they got caught. I wasn't worried about it. In the end we brought the bullets back to Dubai and sold each bullet for five Indian rupees. I had bought them for almost nothing. For the crew though, it wasn't like pearl diving when they would get a share.

Life on the boat was better than in the pearl diving days – you couldn't even compare. The boats were still wooden with a sail, but bigger and more comfortable. Life remained hard though. Once on our way to India we were caught in a big storm. The wind and water were in my eyes and one eye became very irritated and painful. When I got to India it was hurting

We had heard about oil being discovered in Kuwait, Saudi, Bahrain and Abu Dhabi so we were waiting to see about Dubai. We were thinking, "Why not here?"

When Sheikh Rashid broke the news to us that oil had been found we were extremely happy, of course. Sheikh Rashid used the oil money to develop Dubai. I went to the opening ceremony when they took the first big tank, to collect the oil, a *Khazzan* and sank it to the bottom of the sea. It was built in Jumeirah on the beach. (3)

so much I went to the doctor to stop the pain. He said he could stop the pain, but that I would lose my eye. I told him to stop the pain. Thank God it was only one eye!

The gold trade with India started during the Second World War. It was the Kuwaitis who started this first. They would collect the gold from people here and someone would take it to Kuwait and then on to India from there. People here learned the way of gold trading and in the end it became bigger in Dubai. The gold traders had the gold in a vest inside their clothes and then they put a jacket over the top to take it ashore. Sometimes the Dubai boats would wait offshore and Indian boats would come to collect the gold. Then the Indians would put on the vests.

Once, in Bombay, in the early 1950s, our boat was boarded. I was on land but the crew was asked who the boat belonged to. My name was mentioned. When I got the news I felt unsafe so I decided to leave. It was late Friday. I had some gold and cash in a safe deposit box in India, but I had to wait until Monday to get it. I decided to stay with friends.

When I had the money I took a train to Delhi and stayed quiet for a while hoping the situation would get better. When I came back to Bombay I called my friends here and each one put down the phone, as a signal when they heard my voice. I decided to go to Calcutta thinking that if I could get to East Pakistan (2) by train I could reach Karachi by plane.

My passport had expired. When the Indian border guard saw that, I gave him 100 rupees, but he didn't give me an exit stamp. That meant when I got to the East Pakistani side they told me to go back to the Indian side. When the train started moving back, I jumped off and began running. The guards chased me so I ran into the woods. I rested under a tree – I didn't know where I was. I was sure they would catch me if I tried to cross the border.

I started walking with a family I met and they went to a different checkpoint where the guards couldn't read. The guards saw I had some rupees and asked me where I wanted to go. They pointed me to a different railway station. I got a ticket and made it to East Pakistan.

I was dirty from running and hiding in the woods. I didn't have any money, but I had wired some to a man before I'd left India so I could get a plane ticket. I went to see him, but the money hadn't arrived. I told the man to take my Parker pen and Rolex watch and give me the money for the ticket, as there was only one seat left. He told me to wait. At last the money came through and I took the flight to Karachi. Once I was there I knew I was alright because I had lots of friends who could help me.

When I got back to Dubai after about three weeks, nobody had known where I was – or if I was alive or dead. I felt like a hero when I came home.

Saif remains at the helm of his family's retail, real estate, manufacturing and investment business as Chairman of the Al Ghurair Group.

1. See Chapter 4, 'The Loyal Companion'.
2. East Pakistan became Bangladesh in 1971. Before then East and West Pakistan formed a single entity, although geographically separated by India.
3. See Chapter 21, 'The Industrialist'

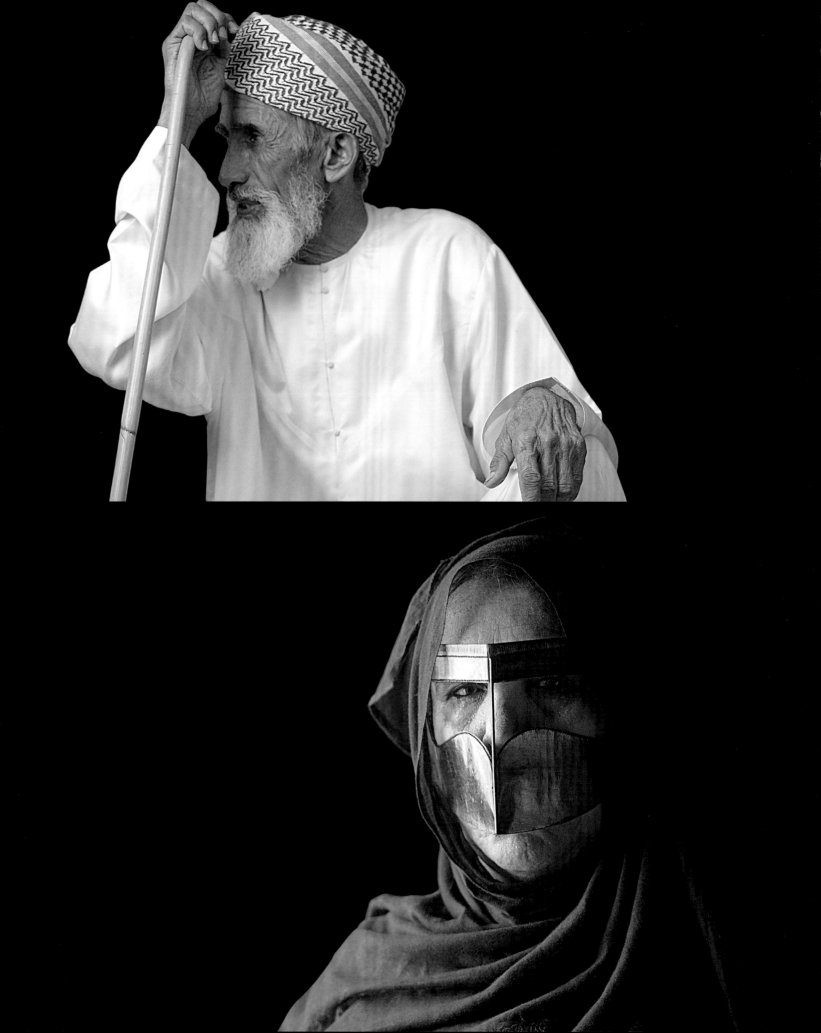

Old friends

HUMAID ALI OBAID AL RAZI

AYESHA SALEM KHALFAN AL KETBI

TRANSLATED BY THEIR FRIENDS, SUAD IBRAHIM DARWISH & AHMED AL WARDI

My mother told me I was born in Umm Al Qaiwain. I don't know which year. Back then, Bedouin people travelled around so babies were born wherever the family was at the time. I was born in a tent. For all Bedouin people, life started in a tent. We call it a *bayt al shaar*.

Life was hard in those days. We had two months here, two months there. We moved from Umm Al Qaiwain to Dubai, to Al Awir, Al Khawaneej, Sharjah, Al Badiyah and Mushrif. These were the places where we knew we would get water. In some places the water was more sweet and in other places it was more salty. Some of the best water was in Al Awir and Al Badiyah. In the summer we would stay in one place for three months. After that, when the weather changed we moved on. Everybody went by a camel – even pregnant women. Our life was based around the camels.

We ate bread, and dates from Basra in Iraq – as there were no date palms in the desert here. Until I was ten I didn't see rice, only flour for bread. There were hares in the desert and also migrating birds like houbara.

We would leave the old men to take a rest in the tents and the young men would go to the *souq*. The *souq* in Dubai was in Al Arsa, in Bur Deira, where the Old Souq is now. People came from all over – some from Oman by camel which would take one month. Everybody came here. We called Dubai the eye of the world. We brought grass and wood from the desert and butter made from the milk of our animals. We sold these and then bought the things we needed. When there wasn't any coffee we took grain, heated it on the fire with water and drank it like coffee. (1)

When we came to Dubai to buy food and things for the home we would buy a little more than our family needed. When we came home to the tents the mothers or fathers would call their sons and daughters and give them food to take to other families. All Bedouin people shared like this.

I went to Dammam in Saudi Arabia when I was 20 to earn money. I went there by boat. I was a worker with the builders – I carried the *jus*. Later I went to Kuwait and worked in a house there for a lady. I saved money and with this money I got married.

Back in Dubai I had a car, a Land Rover, and I took people to Oman and many places – like a taxi. I would take one person from Dubai to near Muscat for about ten rupees. There were no roads, just sand. There were two tracks, one for cars like the Land Rover, one for big vehicles like Bedford trucks. One time we came from Salalah and we took the way near Hatta. The car was very old and we had too many things inside so we had a problem. The car stopped and we stayed there seven days. There were British soldiers there and they gave us food and water. I was with a family, with ladies. We slept outside, there were no mattresses – just we slept on the ground.

Many people my age have forgotten what it was like back then. I remember – our life was very difficult.

I knew Ayesha when she was young. She was strong, very strong and she would fight with me. Ayesha lived with her father and mother. She cooked, worked and did everything they wanted her to do. She is a Bedouin. A good Bedouin girl respects her family and cannot do anything without permission. She cannot go outside her home without asking her father or mother.

When she came to my house I said to my mother, "Why did you let Ayesha come to our house? Tell her to go out because she will take my things and eat my sweets," but my mother said "No, she is good." Still to this time she loves Ayesha.

I was born in a tent in a place named Mirdif. I don't know when. I don't know how old I am, maybe 55, maybe more or maybe less. All the families stayed in tents. Some people had seven, eight, nine, ten people in a tent. For me, there was my mother and father, my brother, sister and me. My uncle and aunt moved around with us. Between five and 30 families would be together in a group, but people would come and go. We would move to find a green area for our animals to graze. We had camels, goats and sheep.

I met Humaid in Khawaneej when we were small. We played together, we talked, we shouted together. He was like a brother. Sometimes when we fought he would hit me and I would go to my family crying.

In the summer we all came together close to a well and some *ghaff* trees. In the winter we moved around more. When we pitched our tents we put the opening facing the breeze so it kept us cool. We never put our tents near the sea – this place was not for the Bedouin people. We put the door so that it wasn't opposite another house, but a little bit to the side so the ladies could come and go without anyone seeing.

When a place became dirty, we moved on. We had animals so after about two months we would need a clean place. Our family didn't move too far like some people, just from Mirdif to Mushrif or Khawaneej.

We brought water from Abu Hail. We put the water in the *girab*. We would take four or five to our house. We ate bread, meat, mutton and camel's milk.

As a family we sat together, but if people came from outside the men sat out in the *majlis*. The ladies sat in the tent. I started to wear a *burqa* when I became a woman. I wore it when we had guests, but not when I was with only my family.

I helped my mother make the *bayt al shaar*. She taught me how to do tailoring – how to make a *thoub*, a *kandoura* and a *burqa*. My mother taught me how to make food and how to make things from leather. We made *girab* for the water, rice and meat. Sometimes we used salt to keep the meat for a long time. The salt came from Dubai, from the end of The Creek – Ras Al Khor.

For marriage, the family of a boy would look for a girl near to them. They would go direct to the family to tell them, "We need your daughter for our son." Before they gave an answer the girl's family would see if any cousin needed the girl for marriage. If he did, he would take her. The cousin had priority.

My husband was from outside the family, from the Bani Yas tribe. I was 12 years old when I got married. I hadn't seen my husband before. I didn't feel anything. I wasn't nervous. I wasn't thinking. I was small, only 12 years old. All I was used to was playing outside. I wasn't asked if I wanted to marry him or not. If they had asked me I would have told them yes. I could not tell them no, because I was afraid of my father.

The day I got married was the best day of my life. My mother was very happy. For the mothers, the important thing was the girls – they cared about them so much. When I got married, my mother was happy because I was settled. At my wedding there was a local band, called *Al Razfa*. There was lots of food – we slaughtered a camel for the feast and many people came to my wedding.

My husband's father and mother had passed away, so we put my husband's tent near to my family. We only slept there, but we went to my family's tent to eat.

I was around 15 when I had my first child. I lost my first baby girl because I had carried a heavy thing when I was pregnant. The last boy died too. I have six children now. When the babies came my mother was with me to help. At this time there was a new hospital, Al Maktoum Hospital, (2) but we were scared of the doctor. We didn't know this doctor, although we had heard about him. I didn't need this doctor – I had my mother. My husband was there too. He held me up from behind when the baby was coming – this was normal. My husband talked to me and gave me some words to relax. He cut the cord of the baby with a knife.

After the babies were born there was some Arabic medicine which I took for three days. It was like an oil and there was also some medicine that was spicy. I mixed it, drank it and it cleaned my stomach. After this there was no pain, nothing, and I felt good. We used salt water to wash ourselves. I fed my babies myself for two years.

When the baby was coming out we didn't take any medicine – nothing. The ladies before were not crying like now. Before they were strong. Two or three days after the baby was born I started to work – cooking, everything. Life went on. Thank God.

Humaid and Ayesha work alongside one another at Dubai's Heritage Village in Shindagha demonstrating how the Bedouin used to live.

1. Barley coffee. Date stones were also dried, ground and mixed with water and spices to drink instead of coffee.
2. Al Maktoum Hospital opened in Deira in 1949. Father of Dubai, Wilson, 1999, p.74.

61

CHAPTER 9

The Dhow Builder

SAIF MOHAMMED AL QAIZI

TRANSLATED BY HIS FRIEND, SALAH BIN TOUQ

I was born in Umm Hurair, Dubai in about 1928. My father worked as a dhow carpenter. He died when I was nine or ten years old and afterwards I started the same job. I had five sisters, no brothers. I was the youngest, but I was the only man. In those days, we boys went to learn The Koran in the morning and evening, but after my father died no one had the money to pay for school so I left.

In the summer I went pearl diving. Over the years I did all the jobs on the dive. I started as a boy and I used to fetch things – water, dates and food. Next, I started opening the shells and then I was a *saib* – the man who pulled up the rope. Then I became a diver. We were young boys and healthy – we were happy, but the captains were very strong and strict. At that time if you didn't go diving you would have no money – there was no other work. This money was for food for my family. My father had died so there was no other choice.

On the dhow we smoked a *narilla* as there were no cigarettes then. A *narilla* was a coconut shell brought from India and cleaned inside. On one side we made a hole for tobacco, on the other we put a small pipe and sucked it like *shisha*. We would smoke when we came up from diving, when we were resting in the sea and before going down again. One *narilla* was passed around between the divers.

The water was 12 to 14 metres deep. We had a peg to close our nose and a weight on our feet of maybe eight to ten kilogrammes made from zinc which came from India. The weight took us down quickly. When we needed to come up we tugged on the rope and the *saib* pulled us up.

The year was split into two sections. Part of the year was spent diving, the rest, when the water was cooler, people would go travelling for trade. They would go to Iraq to load the dates in Basra, then to India to unload them, then from India to Africa to take more things. Then they would come back for a few days or a few weeks before starting again. This was the life.

'The smugglers had cash and they weren't interested in how much it would cost to repair the boats.'

In the winter I worked as a carpenter repairing the dhows for the pearling, fishing and trading people. The workshop was in Al Ras. To get there I rowed my own small boat from Umm Hurair to Bur Deira. Then I left it on the sand and walked to Al Ras. Back then, all the families in Dubai had dhows, big, medium or small, and people got their food from the sea. My cousin, Musabah, started to teach me how to be a dhow carpenter and later I slowly taught myself how to built the boats.

I was so happy when the hard work of diving had finished for the year and I started my carpentry. It meant in the evenings I would be in the town. I would be able to enjoy the weddings, the dancing and the parties. In the middle of the sea there was no chance for this. We built new boats, repaired older boats, checked nails, changed the keels and put cotton in the space between the wood. At that time we worked by the day. Every day I got one rupee – it was very little money. My cousin was happy because he had a healthy boy to help him. Each lunchtime the owner of the boat would bring us food, usually from his house, and each evening he would bring us our wage.

For most of the boats we used teak wood outside and *qarat* inside. The teak came from India, but there were merchants in Dubai who sold it. You could go to the man who had the teak wood and he trusted you. You took the wood and when the owner of the boat paid you, you went back to pay for the wood. The same happened with the nails which we got from the blacksmiths working near Al Ras.

In the 1960s I would go to Oman to buy *qarat* wood for building dhows. I went to the big gardens there and I would check the trees to see how many bends they had. I was the

carpenter so I chose the wood. I knew which piece would go on the front and which piece would go on the back or down the side. I could look at the trees and see that – the design was in my head. I would tell the people where to cut so that we didn't lose a single foot.

I would stay in Oman for two months and after cutting these trees we would bring them back overland on Bedford trucks. Before, there were no roads between here and Oman – it was just sand so it was not easy to drive. It was so hot as there was no air conditioning in the trucks, so we would wear only our underwear when we were driving, no *kandoura*.

We moved our boatyard up The Creek as the city grew. We started in Al Ras, but we had to move near to Dubai Municipality, then Umm Hurair and later Jaddaf.

The first bigger boat I built was called 'Matara'. *Matar* means rain and Matara is a woman's name. I named it that because it was raining at the time we built that dhow.

When the gold smuggling stopped in Kuwait some carpenters who had been working there came here looking for a job. In the end, 14 Omanis worked for me building boats. This was in the 1950s and 1960s when there was lots of gold smuggling. The smugglers had cash and they weren't interested in how much it would cost to repair the boats, but they needed it done quickly so they could make more trips to India. We stopped using the diving boats and brought some faster boats from Pakistan – boats with engines. We would work 24 hours a day building new boats and fixing two or three engines on boats that would take gold from Dubai to India.

The smugglers were nearly all from the Deira side. I would fix the engines sometimes within six hours and they would load the gold on the boats and then they would go to India again. At that time there were around 100 to 120 boats going from here to India.

Once I bought 300,000 rupees of gold. After two weeks it was worth 600,000 and the smugglers asked me if I needed the money back or if I would smuggle again. I said I would do it again, but after one month they told me the dhow and the gold had gone. I lost it all.

The work was secret. Nobody was meant to know what time the gold was loaded or what time the boats sailed. The owner of the gold had good communications with India and they would know if, for example, on the 28th of the month there would be a festival. That meant the police and the coastguard would be busy and it was a good time to smuggle the gold. Some people here watched the boats and they would call the Indian police to tell them a boat with a particular number was on its way with gold. The smugglers had to be very careful.

Often the gold was kept in small boxes and when the smugglers came near the coast of India,

'The work was secret. Nobody was meant to know what time the gold was loaded or what time the boats sailed.'

they would break the boxes and put them in special belts which went around their middle. An Indian boat would come out to the Dubai boat and they'd have a special code. Sometimes when the smugglers reached the coast the Indian fishing boat wouldn't come out – maybe because of the weather or the police on the shore. Then the smugglers might wait for a few days until the fishing boat came or if it didn't come they'd bring the gold back.

At this time we worked very hard, but we earned a lot of money. We didn't sleep, we only worked. It was such a difference to the difficult times before. I built a new house and I married two ladies. Lots of people had lots of money in their pockets. It was a golden time. We thought it would last for ever.

Saif continues to design and build boats from his own boatyard in Jaddaf on The Creek.

CHAPTER 10

The Migrant Worker

MOHAMMAD ABDULRAHIM AL GHAFFARI

TRANSLATED BY HIS COUSIN, MOHAMMAD GHAFFARI

I was born in 1933 in Al Buteen, Dubai, near the Naif area in Deira. Our house was made of date palm branches – all of Dubai's houses were like this at the time. There were ten people in my house – three girls and five boys plus our parents. I was the eldest brother. I went to Al Ahmadiya School.

Water used to come by donkey – in jerry cans from a well in Hamriya. The rich people and all the women would bathe in their homes, but the less fortunate men would either go to the sea to wash or to Hamriya, to the well. The soaps would be in blocks which came from India.

My father had a shop in the souq on the Deira side. It was like a grocery shop and sold rice, sugar, tea and so on. People used to come to the area from far away – from Buraimi and other places in Oman. The Bedouin would bring things like grass and wood to sell and would buy supplies like coffee and sugar. I remember when I was around 15 years old I was given the choice either to go diving for pearls or to work in the shop for three rupees a month. I chose the shop.

In the 1940s there was also the chance to work at the old Dubai airport, pouring sand to build the runway. People would register with a British company in Baniyas Square and then they would be hired for half a rupee a day. People would walk to the airport to work. I did this for five days, but it was a very long way from Deira so I didn't go back after that.

Later, towards the end of the Second World War, I started working in the RAF base in Sharjah (1) and stayed there for two or three years. At first, my job was to fill up the planes with fuel. I had a green uniform. It was a good job. Outside the base people would be paid half a rupee – inside I got one and a half rupees. The fuel came from Abadan in Iran from the BP (2) oil fields there. It came by barge once a week and Khansaheb was the dealer in Dubai.

'I was given the choice either to go diving for pearls or to work in the shop for three rupees a month. I chose the shop.'

Later I served food in the RAF mess. People from different places used to come to work at the base – men from Iran, Yemen, Jordan, India and so on. It was a big base and it had good facilities – when Dubai and Sharjah didn't have electricity, the RAF base had electricity and fans for cooling.

I used to stay in a house in Sharjah with some relatives. My friends and I would pay one rupee to go to Dubai in a car – I would come back once a week, on a Friday, to see my family.

After working at the RAF base I went to Kuwait to work for KOC, the Kuwait Oil Company. It was in 1948 at the time of the first war in Palestine. I travelled there by boat and it took three days. The trip cost 50 rupees, including food on the way. I went first and then one of my brothers followed. A lot of people from Dubai went to Kuwait at that time – and from Sharjah, Abu Dhabi and Ras Al Khaimah. There was little work in our area and I went there because I knew I could earn more money – we were paid four or five rupees a day which was a lot back then.

I had a certificate from the RAF base in Sharjah to recommend me and at first I worked in the oil company restaurant serving food. Later I became a drill man, drilling for oil on the rigs for an American company called Aminoil. It was very hard, physical work. We would be drilling 2,500 or 3,000 metres underground. It was while I was working on the oil rigs that a heavy piece of equipment fell on my finger. At first I thought it would be fine and I just covered it with a cloth, but it turned purple and was still painful after a week. When I went to the hospital the American doctors said the flesh had died and that it had gangrene so they would have to chop it off. Of course I didn't want that and it took two of them to calm me down and convince me. Eventually I agreed, but although they gave me an injection I could still feel the pain when they did the operation. I still remember that pain.

We had a good life with better conditions in Kuwait than in Dubai and we were very happy. We lived in big white tents with four people in each one. We had beds to sleep on. I shared my tent with other Gulf people. The weather was cooler and there was electricity. The Kuwaitis were happy for us to be there. We felt we were part of one family. We worked for eight hours a day, six days a week with Fridays off. On Fridays we'd just see what was happening and maybe go to a party or a wedding. There was a football club there so sometimes we'd watch soccer. Even women would play there at that time.

It was very safe in Kuwait then. No-one used to steal because the punishment was being lashed and having salt water thrown on you. People used to be afraid to steal.

The only means of communication with Dubai was by letter. There were lots of people from our area in Kuwait so I didn't feel lonely. I would come back to Dubai for a holiday once every two years for two months at a time. When I came back I didn't notice any changes – it was only in the 1960s that things began to change in Dubai.

'When I was in Kuwait I worked with Yasser Arafat. We didn't think he was anything special – he was normal.'

When I was in Kuwait I worked with Yasser Arafat. A lot of Palestinians went to Kuwait for work at that time. He was a civil engineer and he stayed a few years. We didn't think he was anything special – he was normal, I didn't hear him talk about politics and he just seemed to be like any other foreign worker.

When I came back after 15 years in Kuwait I bought my own shop in Dubai with the money I had saved and I got married. I have four sons and three daughters.

I had gone to Kuwait to earn money, save up and come back. It's what many people from all over the world do in Dubai today. When the oil was discovered in Abu Dhabi people started to move back from Kuwait and work there.

I began work at the Dubai Petroleum Company drilling for oil at sea. I don't know which field it was – back then we went by numbers for the areas we drilled. It was far out in the sea – we would go by helicopter to the area and at night we could see the lights of Iran. At this time we were only looking for oil – before it was known for sure that Dubai had oil. It was different to working on land in Kuwait. At sea we only worked, slept and ate – that's all. Of course when oil was discovered we were very happy.

When I was in Kuwait I used to send money back to Dubai from the British Bank of the Middle East. I did it every time I had a few thousand rupees. I would send it to my uncle's bank account, then my family would take it out of the bank and put it in the safe in their house before investing it. (3) I had it in mind to buy land with this money, but my uncle said I should buy a shop with it because land was so cheap and he didn't think it was a good investment. He would ask me, "Why do you want to buy land?" I was in Kuwait and could see how it had been modernised and how the price of land had become higher and higher. I knew the same thing was going to happen to Dubai, but my uncle said it was better to buy a shop. My uncle was like my father; I couldn't say no to him – I had to listen. I wasn't happy about it. The truth is I am still unhappy about it today, but now life is not so hard, there is money, we have everything we need. I do regret listening to my uncle though – if I hadn't I might have been a big millionaire by now. (4)

'I had gone to Kuwait to earn money. It's what many people from all over the world do in Dubai today.'

Mohammad is retired and lives in Al Mezhar in Dubai with his wife and children.

1. RAF Sharjah opened in 1940.
2. British Petroleum.
3. See Chapter 15, 'The Banker'.
4. See Chapter 14, 'The Civil Servant'.

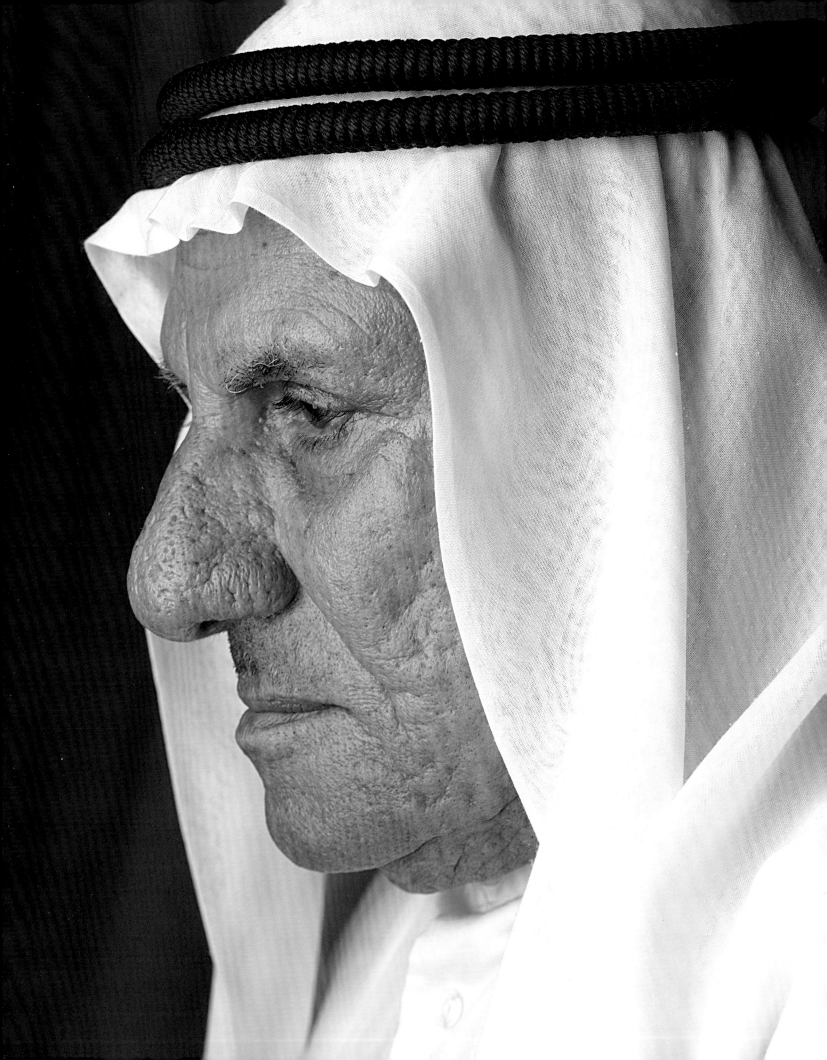

The Medicine Man

DR MOHAMMED SHAREIF AL MULLA

I was born here. It was a little more or a little less than 1930 or 1935. My grandfather was trading in Iran – but he is buried in Dubai. A lot of people used to come and go to Lingah for business. Our house was in Al Bastakia area which is a very old area. Before, it was only Al Bastakia and Al Shindagha on that side. At that time, mostly people lived in houses made from *barasti*.

I left Dubai and went to Bahrain in 1946 or 1947 to work in the Bahrain Petroleum Company, Bapco. I worked with the medical doctors and trained there. Then, in 1951, I went to Saudi Arabia, to Dammam. At that time there was nothing, it was all desert. I worked with the Saudi government as a doctor until 1955 and then I returned to Dubai. Dubai was the land of happiness for everyone.

I opened a pharmacy and clinic where the Gold Souq is now. There was no gold market then, only Sikkat Al Khail. It means Horse Street. Rich people like Sheikh Mohammed Ahmad Bin Dalmook used to ride through this street. This Sheikh was the richest Arab man in Dubai and he was related to the rulers. His house was on the corner where the Municipality Library is now. All year round he would give his *Zakat* to the poor people.

I opened my clinic in Deira because there were more people in Deira. The Bedouin came to this side of The Creek – they would bring butter and wood for the fire from the desert to the Arsa area to sell. At that time the owner of the shop was Abdullah Jaffa and the building cost 250 rupees per year in rent. In that area there were only Omani people making *khanjars* and silver jewellery – there was no gold then. Later, one man came from Bahrain, an Indian called Harry Lal and he opened a gold shop.

There was another pharmacist and the man was a doctor as well. They called him Mohammed Habib Al Reza. He had a place in Bur Dubai and one in Deira. He was a very old friend of the ruler.

'There were hundreds of worms inside but the water was good and no one was sick from it.'

My clinic was a pharmacy on one side and a clinic on the other. I saw ladies and men and I used to deliver babies as well. I would go from place to place. For that reason everybody in Dubai knows me.

If I visited a house it cost five rupees, injections were five rupees and medicine didn't cost much. Back then, if you had ten rupees it was plenty. Not like now. You could buy a big piece of land for 1,000 to 2,000 rupees. We paid the houseboy about five rupees a month. You could buy a sheep for one and a half rupees.

People didn't have too many problems. They came to me with a cough, fever, boils, malaria – not too much. There was measles, and chicken pox in the children. We didn't have any vaccinations – we didn't even have very many medicines. I used to order them from Bahrain. At that time although there wasn't that much medicine it was more effective than now. At first there were no patients. Sometimes I would have just one a day.

I used to go to Umm Al Qaiwain and stay there 15 or 20 days because there were more Bedouin there and it was busier.

In the beginning people here used only fire and local medicine to cure things. If you had stomach pain they would make a mixture to pass things out. Once patients started coming to the clinic though, they did use what I gave them.

I would treat the royal family at their house. I treated all the teachers at the schools and it all went on the account of the Government of Dubai. Ahmed Moosa was the head of the Ruler's Court at the time and he would write a chit to say, 'Please treat this man'. It was very cheap – only four rupees. Other people – from The Municipality or special guards – would also bring a chit from the sheikhs and I would treat them. I have a book with all the details of the people of Dubai that came to me and had an account with me – I would write down what treatment they had and when they had money they would pay me.

I came from my home in the morning and went back for lunch. The same in the afternoon – so I went by *abra* four times a day as there were no roads. I had a special man who rowed me and took me near the *Diwan* and Al Bastakia. At 3.30 in the afternoon he was waiting for me again and he would bring me across. It cost about eight annas – half a rupee.

In the summer, people in Deira went a little way east to the Baraha area. They made *barasti areesh* houses facing the sea so they had fresh air and a well with sweet water. The ladies stayed there and the men came back into the town to work, either by donkey or on foot.

The water came by donkey every day – sometimes, if it was a big house, it came more than once a day. The water was very cheap, for one month maybe five or six rupees. Every house had a well inside which was not sweet and they used it for washing plates. For cooking and rinsing clothes we used sweet water. There were hundreds of worms inside, but the water was good and no one was sick from it.

After Sheikh Rashid, I was the next person to buy a generator. We started it from six o'clock sundown to nearly 12 o'clock in the night. There was no air conditioning, only a fan. Also, I had one of the first televisions. I brought it from Bahrain. The only station we had was from Aramco (1) in Saudi Arabia. Sometimes we got a clear picture, sometimes not. All the people came to see what the box with the pictures was. Aramco had mostly films in English – I remember a lot of Perry Mason (2). It was very good.

After Naif there was nothing, only desert. You can still see the towers we had for lookouts – there is one at the end of Al Shindagha Tunnel, one in Muraqqabat and one near the Baraha Hospital. These were the end of the city. If you passed these in the night the guards would said "Hoi" and you would say "Hoi" – they wanted to know who you were. If you didn't give an answer they would shoot you! It was to keep bad people out of the town. These guards were Bedouin people loyal to the ruler.

We didn't have a Municipality. If you wanted to build a house, Abdullah bin Yamaan would come with a man and he would measure the area and you could build your house. If you wanted to drive you went to see Hasher Al Ghaith in Al Sabkha. He wrote on a piece of paper and you put the note in the car. You didn't need to have a registration card or anything.

'Back then, if there was a complaint between two people they would go to the ruler.'

There were no petrol stations. Gargash was the agent for the petrol and he had a drum – they used a handle and a bottle was on the top to fill it up. There was only one place – Al Sabkha on Deira side. The first road I remember was from Sheikh Ahmed bin Ali Al Thani of Qatar's house – the big one by the Maktoum Bridge – to the Ruler's Office, the *Diwan*, on The Creek.

We didn't have telephones. I remember when the telephone company brought loudspeakers to the *souq* and told every one about the telephones. It started on the Deira side. Then they put up cable and it went to the Dubai side through The Creek.

Before, in Ramadan you would invite people to eat with you. Three or four houses would bring food and put a mat out to eat together. If somebody passed and you didn't know him you would tell him to sit down and eat with you.

Some people went for *Hajj* by ship to Aden, then to Jeddah in the Red Sea and then on to Mecca. Some people went by camel and it took months. From here, mostly we went to Bahrain and from there to Saudi Arabia and Mecca. I went first in 1958 or 1959. I went from here to Bahrain, in a small aircraft to Dammam and on to Jeddah in a Viscount aircraft. Then we went to Mecca. When people came back from *Hajj* there was a celebration. Every house in the area of that family would put out green flags and they called all the pilgrims Hajj – Hajj Abdullah, Hajj Mohammed.

Back then, if there was a complaint between two people they would go to the ruler. He or his man would listen to the story. If you could settle it, you settled it. If not, he would send you to the judge – there were three judges here.

For nearly 45 years I went to Sheikh Rashid at Zabeel early every morning except Friday and if I didn't go he would ask where I was. We would sit and talk and take coffee. He was always asking, "What is the news?" He always wanted to know what was going on. One day I had an accident and the next day he asked me about it before I told him it had happened! Sheikh Rashid was a doctor, a ruler, a teacher – everything. He didn't do things for himself, but only to help the people. If you came to him and you needed something, he wouldn't say anything, but after two or three days he would tell you, "OK." Sheikh Rashid was a great man.

In the old days all the people would help each other. If someone was sick, everybody would go to his house in the morning and evening to see how he was. Nowadays everyone is running after money. They have billions of dirhams, but still it is not enough.

Dr Shareif continues to work from his clinic in the Gold Souk each day,
now crossing The Creek by road from his house in Jumeirah.

1. Saudi Arabian Oil Company, based in Dhahran.
2. American courtroom drama series.

CHAPTER 12

The Policeman

BRIGADIER GENERAL KHALIFA BIN DHAIN AL MUHAIRI

TRANSLATED BY HIS COLLEAGUES, WARRANT OFFICER KHALID ABDULLA SAEED AL MAZROUI
AND SERGEANT AHMED IDRIS ADAM

I was born in Jumeirah Number 1. I don't know exactly which year as there was no registration at that time. My father was a pearl diver. It was a very temporary life as well as a poor one. I had 12 brothers and two sisters. I was the sixth child.

In summer the family went to Al Ain because it was very hot in Dubai. We came back to Jumeirah for the winter. Life was difficult. People were living in houses made from palm branches. There was no work and we needed money to live so when I was 16, I went to register at Dubai Police. It was 1956.

'Before me there were only seven people in Dubai Police. I was number eight.'

Before me there were only seven people in Dubai Police. I was the eighth, my brother was the ninth and my friend, Mohammed Khalfan, was the tenth. We went to Naif in Deira, to a very old building like a fort – in the same place as Naif Police Station is now. There was no invitation, but we went willingly – we had heard about the army and the police abroad and we wanted to be like them. When I started I earned 120 Indian rupees a month.

There was no uniform – we wore a white *kandoura* with a red material belt which crossed over our chests, and a red *khizam*. At first we just had a truncheon then later a rifle with five bullets each. We had some marching training with a sergeant major from Oman, but there wasn't training about how to be a good policeman – we just knew what was wrong and what was right and we

tried to prevent people from doing the wrong things. Everyday we did two shifts of six hours each in the *souqs*, one morning and one night shift. We worked from six in the morning until noon and then from ten at night to four in the morning. Some of us were in Bur Dubai and some in Deira and there were two or three patrols at one time, each with one person. The *souqs* closed after sunset and our duty was to stop people going inside them.

At about four o'clock one morning we received a report that two people had been killed behind Al Fahidi Fort. I was a lance corporal. My boss was a sergeant, a Pakistani. We went there and found two people whose stomachs had been slit open. I told my colleagues I could track the culprits by following their footprints in the sand, but they were afraid to go because we didn't have guns and we didn't know how many people had committed the crime. It was still dark but I decided to go by myself. I had only a truncheon. I followed the track which went from Al Fahidi Fort to Jumeirah and then to Jebel Ali – past where the Jebel Ali Hotel is now. It was in the morning at about nine o'clock when I found the criminal there. He

was tired. I was tired, but I was strong – I liked the dangerous cases and I was determined. I was always willing to catch criminals. When I saw this man I picked up my truncheon like a rifle and he believed it was a gun. I told him to turn around and I used my *khizam* to tie him up. I brought him back to Dubai before *Maghrib* prayers. When I got back the captain kissed my head.

I had had experience of following the tracks of camels and my friends' footprints when I was young. From some tracks you can see the toes are bent to the inside, some have the toes apart and some toes are shorter than others. I still do this tracking for Dubai Police now. Before, when somebody was arrested they were taken to a cell at Naif Police Station in Deira. When they were found guilty they were brought back to Naif, to the same jail and they stayed there until they had finished their sentence.

The police didn't have cars then, but there were horses for the officers who patrolled on the outskirts – in Jumeirah or the dunes.

At first people looked at policemen as strangers and they didn't accept or like them. Officers couldn't go inside Jumeirah because it was an area for local Bedouin people. The Bedouin didn't like any strangers and they were strong-minded. The police were a new thing and they came from here and there – from Jordan, Bahrain and other places, but when the Bedouin's children went to register with the police they came to understand what it meant and slowly it got better.

A Jordanian captain who was working in

Qatar began training us and from that day on we wore a uniform. It was green trousers, a shirt and beret and a smaller badge than now. We started doing some marching from Bur Dubai to Jumeirah Number 4 with music – there was a band with trumpets and drums. People gathered and they all liked it a lot.

One night I was patrolling in Bur Dubai when I saw two men with small bags. I asked them to stop, but they ran away so I chased them. One tried to climb over the wall to a compound and I caught his leg. He dropped the bag, but took out his knife and slashed my arm right across. I tried to hold on to him, but I couldn't because the pain was too much. I climbed the wall and jumped inside the area to try to catch him. He got away, but some blood from my cut had stuck to his back. When I looked in the bag there were 200 Rolex watches from Ahmed Seddiqui's shop. I asked the owner of the compound to witness the number of watches in the bag as they were very valuable.

I tried to bandage my arm with a poultice of salt and turmeric to stop it bleeding. Then I took three policemen and went to the compound. There were no tracks outside so I knew he was there. People started gathering there to find out what was happening. Then I saw my blood on one man's back and I knew it was the man I had chased. We found there were 400 stolen watches altogether.

After I had arrested the criminals I went to see Dr McCaully at the Maktoum Hospital (1) and he put my arm in a sling. Sheikh Maktoum called me to his *majlis* because he was angry. He said, "If I didn't see your arm hurting I would hit you with my stick. Why do you chase criminals without rifles or guns? You might be killed." I told him that it is my job and my duty to prevent criminals from committing crimes in my country. If I am killed in this duty, so be it.

I am a policeman and I believe in what I do – in my heart. I believe in my God. In Islam, if you don't do your job properly you shouldn't get your money. This is what I learned at a very young age from my family. I decided when I joined the police I would do my duty properly for my country and the rulers.

One Indian, known as Banyan (2), who had a shop in Souq Al Banyan in Bur Dubai, left his shop and his safe open one night. I went there and saw there was no one inside. There were rows of 50 rupee notes and 10s below. I called my friend and showed him. He joked we should bring a big bag, but I told him to do his job. I waited there until the Indian came running. I asked him to check the safe and make sure it was all there. The man is still in Dubai and whenever he sees me he always kisses my head.

The local people were very honest and tried to solve their problems – they were poor, but trustworthy – they believed in their religion.

Once I was patrolling in Hor Al Anz in a Land Rover. We were told that one person had some drugs. The criminal was driving a water tanker with Ajman registration plates. We tried to stop the tanker but the criminal tried to crash into us. There were no roads, just sand. We were getting near Sharjah and we couldn't cross the border – it was a crime for Dubai Police to chase someone into Sharjah. I told my driver to pull alongside the tanker and I shot the man behind his ear. He stopped and we arrested him.

When I came back, Mr Briggs (3) asked why I shot him. He said he hadn't ordered me to do that, but I told him I couldn't let him get inside Sharjah. He said I could have killed the man and he suspended me from duty for seven days. Then there was a court martial with Mr Briggs.

'..we couldn't cross the border – it was a crime for Dubai Police to chase someone into Sharjah'

He asked me, "Aren't you guilty?" I told him I wasn't because I was preventing people from committing bad crimes. He said I couldn't have a gun anymore. I was trying my best – I didn't want to kill the criminals, but just to stop them. For the commanders though, they thought it was dangerous, even though on a different occasion, another officer, Mr Humphreys, said in other countries I would have been thought of as a hero.

We respected our commanders wherever they came from. We were the same force and doing the same job. We all believed in that job. The foreigners were teaching us because they knew better and they were giving us what they knew. When I became a policeman I learned much from these people, so I respected them. We were all doing our duty together. It is the same now with His Highness, Sheikh Mohammed, as our commander. He tells us to treat everyone the same wherever they come from – we are all human beings.

Brigadier General Khalifa is the Director of Nad Al Sheba Police Station

where he oversees the security of the sheikhs' palaces.

1. Lieutenant Colonel Donald McCaully was the Senior Medical Officer for the Trucial States, Father of Dubai, Wilson, 1999, p.17.

2. Name often given to Indian people in Dubai.

3. Jack Briggs, British Commandant of Dubai Police, 1965-75, widely credited with guiding the force through its formative years.

CHAPTER 13

The Determined Scholar

DR HESSAH ABDULLAH BIN HUSSAIN LOOTAH

I was born in Dubai in 1952 or 1953. The town has changed very much since then of course, but we were living in a place close to where the Gold Souq is now. Most of the people lived there at that time. Our house was built with stones brought from the sea, and gypsum. The houses were cool and more suitable for the environment than houses are now.

My grandfather, Hussain Bin Lootah, was famous for being an owner of many pearl ships. He died before I was born, but I heard a lot of stories about him. My father was like a landlord. He was a close friend of Sheikh Rashid and they were together most of the time. They even fought together when there were tribal fights at that time.

I think our school was the first girls' school ever to be opened in Dubai. (1) It was called Al Khansaa and named after an old Arab poet known for being courageous and brave. The school was in what was at that time Sheikha Shamsa bint Sultan's house. She was the mother of Sheikha Latifa bint Hamdan who was the late Sheikh Rashid's wife. When they opened the school we were very happy, my older sister and I. At the beginning the teachers were Palestinians and later there were some Egyptians. Educated people were very respected by the people here. We did many subjects – History, Classical Arabic, Geography, Science and lots of activities.

My sister stayed for one year and then my family took her out of school. I was allowed to stay four years and then I also had to leave. I was about 11 years old. It was the first disaster of my life! At that time a girl's education wasn't looked upon as something necessary, important or even appreciated among the big families. It was my older brother who decided no. My father was still alive at this time so I don't know why my brother was given the privilege of deciding on our lives, but he was our older brother and we had to respect his decision. I think my parents agreed, but they made him the one to spell it out. I was very depressed about the decision. I cried and tried to persuade my family, but all my attempts failed.

'I wanted to do something worthwhile with my life and to unite with other women who had the same interests.'

My outlet was to read everything I could get hold of – books, magazines, everything. That's what kept me going. There was one bookstore in an area near Naif and one in the *souq*. I would call them on the phone, but I wasn't allowed to go out to those areas.

I remember one time I didn't buy clothes with the money I was given for Eid, I bought books instead. I had so much dedication at that time. So many things we read when we were young made the rest of the world very familiar to us – novels from England, Russia, France, even sometimes China. That contributed to me feeling that we are like the rest of the world and to thinking about people everywhere having the same sorrows and happiness.

A group of friends, including my older sister, and I founded the first women's association in Dubai – it was in 1965, I think. I was about 12 or 13 at the time. In that era people were maturing at that age. We taught women how to read and write and organised some social events. The group lasted a few years. It was called 'The Omani Women's Renaissance Association'. Back then the region wasn't separated from Oman, at least in the minds of the people. It was often called the Omani coast so lots of institutions appeared with Oman's name on them.

Then in 1973 I initiated what is now the Dubai Women's Association. (2) I worked on that for several years. We had various programmes, including lectures, literacy programmes, health talks and events. We tried to collaborate with other associations in Bahrain or Kuwait. Also, whenever well known figures came to Dubai we would invite them to speak. There were so many issues at that time in the wider region – there were colonialism issues and liberation issues. We were following these and taking part by trying to move towards the liberation of women. I wanted to do something worthwhile with my life and to unite with other women who had the same interests. We would try to encourage people to get involved with the issues and problems that might happen in society. We wanted to get people to read and be interested in poetry. We were trying to get women together.

A lot of men would send their regards and best wishes to support us and we also received support from Sheikh Maktoum for the first place we rented. We tried to support it financially ourselves and we even cleaned the place ourselves. Whoever had books would donate them to the association. We had a feeling it was ours and we were involved in it full-heartedly. We tried to make a difference in people's lives. There was a sense of solidarity and collaboration – whatever concerned people we tried to highlight it. Certain things changed Dubai. People didn't tend to cross The Creek except for special occasions, but the Maktoum Bridge made life easier for people (3) to get together and created a flow between Dubai and Deira. At first it cost one rupee for every car to cross – it meant people were involved in the services they received.

What really changed people's lives was moving from the older settlements – it changed them negatively in terms of housing and social relationships. When we moved from the *souq* to Naif people there were new for us, but they were mostly local and we got along well. Moving to Al Baraha, close to the Kuwaiti (4) and Dubai hospitals saw life change for us with new areas and people. Then we moved to Al Mamzar; now we don't know our neighbours well. Still, I discovered, talking to my Uncle Saeed, when the Lootah family moved from Abu Dhabi over

Of course, when we were young the family girls would be told not to sit with the servants, but we broke that rule all the time. Servants were treated differently then; at the time when we were in the *souq* area there was a lady with us who was supposedly a slave, but I called her 'My Mother'. Until now when I see her I kiss her head and call her this. I love her and respect her very much.

five generations ago, they settled in Al Mamzar. I told him we are back in our ancestors' place. After I got married, when I was about 19 or 20, evening schools were opened here and later, I went to continue my education in Egypt and America. Of course my brother still didn't agree and we argued, but I decided I would do it anyway. I was about to graduate when some members of my family were involved in a car accident in Dubai and a lot of girls passed away – among them was my brother's daughter and four cousins of mine. It was in January 1983 and it was the first big accident in the Emirates – even Reuters wrote about it. I couldn't continue my studies and I came back.

I started work at Dubai TV. My family didn't reject me going to work there, but at that time it wasn't much appreciated. I was the first woman director there. At that time there were only a few stations to watch and it was a centre in people's lives. I made some pioneering programmes. One was called 'Hadith Al Nas' which means 'Talk of the People' and we dealt with so many issues that weren't talked about publicly then – divorce, drugs, unsafe cars, the increase in expatriates – so many things. When we talked about drugs it was the first time people had heard addicts talk about their experiences and what they had gone through. That was shocking for people; it was an education for them. People started to say the programme had become the talk of the people.

As in all countries, change takes time to be accepted. Over time my brother has changed his opinions and all his daughters are now highly educated – I heard him once telling them, "I want you to be like your aunt."

Hessah completed her PhD in the United States researching the image of women at Dubai TV.

She now teaches at the UAE University in Al Ain.

1. The first girls' schools were established in 1958; Al Khansaa in Deira and Khawla School in Bur Dubai. See Chapter 16, 'The Provider'.
2. See Chapter 19, 'The Volunteer'.
3. Opened 1962, Father of Dubai, Wilson, 1999, p.86.
4. The original name for Al Baraha Hospital.

CHAPTER 14

The Civil Servant

KHALIFA MOHAMMAD AL KHALLAFI

TRANSLATED BY MOHAMMED SULTAN THANI

I was born in the town of Dubai in the area of Deira on September 7th 1945. There were no official birth certificates then, but the fathers usually wrote down when their children were born and they related it to something that had happened – maybe local or international wars.

Part of our house was made of stone and the rest was *areesh*. At first it was only one big room, then we added more rooms and it became a big house. I was the eldest of five children – we were two brothers and three sisters and we all lived in one house in the Al Ras area. Some of my uncles, aunts and my grandfather were also living with us. Most of our neighbours had the same style of house and the same standard of living.

My father owned two pearl diving and fishing boats. He usually stayed in the city, but he also went pearling as a *nokhada*. He was one of the few people whose boats continued with pearl diving at the end of that era. (1)

At that time there was nothing for children to do – only playing around the area and going to school. I went to Al Ahmadiya School. By the 1950s, they had started teaching Maths, Geography, Arabic, even English. I was one of the last people to attend the original Al Ahmadiya.

After I left there, when I was 14 or 15, I went to Qatar to continue my education with lots

of my friends from Dubai. At that time Qatar and Bahrain had a more advanced education system than here. We were on a scholarship and we all knew it was a very good opportunity. We were the first group to go to Qatar from Dubai. My father was proud and he helped me, but it was very difficult to go because my mother didn't agree. She was afraid about me going to another country and because of this I only stayed two years. There were around 15 of us students, all boys, and because we were young we weren't allowed to go further than Qatar, but some of the older boys were sent to Egypt, Iraq and Damascus in Syria.

Sheikh Ahmed bin Ali, the Ruler of Qatar, was married to Sheikh Rashid's daughter, Sheikha Mariam. In our group there was a boy from the Maktoum family and so in the holidays we would go to greet Sheikha Mariam.

The supervisor in Qatar was very tough and he tried to discipline us very strongly so we decided to return to Dubai. When Sheikh Rashid heard about it he requested we visit him. He asked what had happened and we told him. He said, "No, there is nothing, finish, you go back and afterwards I will come there to see." We were only in Dubai for two days before we had to go back, but at least my mother was very happy to see me!

After Qatar I tried to continue my education in Egypt, but because of my mother I was forced to come back. It was in 1961 when, by chance, I went to visit The Land Department just when it was starting. Sheikh Maktoum was there. The people asked me why I had to go to Egypt when I could continue my education in Dubai. I joined the Land Department and later I went for tuition in the afternoons and the Department paid for it.

In the beginning it was very difficult for people to understand the procedure of how to measure the land and record it, but after six months or one year, people would come by themselves to ask to register their land. At that time The Land Department was very small. There was only the President's Office for Sheikh Maktoum, and the manager was Mohammed Adam, a Sudanese man. The other five or six employees were in one big open office and there was one guard.

Sheikh Rashid distributed responsibilities between his sons – Sheikh Maktoum at The Land Department, Sheikh Hamdan at The Municipality and Sheikh Mohammed at Dubai Police. In The Land Department there was a lot of documentation for title deeds and these were usually signed either by Sheikh Rashid or Sheikh Maktoum – he was the eldest son so he was usually responsible for doing this.

When we went to survey lands, usually we took a surveyor from Dubai Municipality. The manager was new here and he didn't know everyone, so there was a committee of people who knew all the homes and the people. The committee was paid money to decide the land area and we went with them to measure it. They would say, "This man's land starts from here and goes to here." There were two groups in the committee, one from Deira and the other from Bur Dubai. They were old men – people who were respected and important in Dubai. Most of the disputes were between neighbours arguing what belonged to whom, but the committee decided there and then and finished the matter. Usually that was it, but if things were too complicated the people would go to the court. Sometimes the committee would bring witnesses to say who they thought owned the land. We

'Most of the disputes were between neighbours arguing what belonged to whom.'

heard about people trying to give money for witnesses to say the land was theirs, but I never saw it myself. Any unclaimed land was registered as belonging to the government until someone came to claim it and brought witnesses.

Out of the town in the farms, when there was a palm tree on the land, the committee would usually give 20 or 30 feet of land around the tree to the person. It was like a border. Even if there was only the remains of the tree, we considered it part of the farm. At some farms the father had passed away and the children might have been very young so they didn't know who owned the land. Then it was up to the neighbours to tell us what they remembered. There were many funny things that happened. In the Abu Hail area we went to survey a plot where a man had three palm trees. It became dark so we said we would come back in two days to finish the job. When we came back there were four palm trees. We asked him where the fourth one had come from. He told us, "It is very old." When we touched it, it fell down!

There wasn't a resistance among the people about registering the land because it meant they then had official documentation for what they owned. Before, there was nothing like this. Some people complained about the decisions of the committee because they thought they should be given more land.

'Nobody wanted the land where Sheikh Zayed Road and the Trade Centre are now – it was very cheap. '

Many people in Dubai would come to The Land Department in the morning and use it as a meeting place, especially when we were at the old building near where The Municipality is now. There was a big lobby and some people would buy and sell land, but lots came just to meet each other and greet friends. Sheikh Maktoum was always there and everyone would come to greet him. It wasn't only land that was talked about.

There were very few people who crossed The Creek to live, but they went for visits. Sometimes there was a marriage between families from either side and in this case it would be the wife who came to live on the other side of The Creek. Before the Maktoum Bridge was built (2) if you wanted to go by car you had to go to the top of The Creek, to Ras Al Khor, or otherwise use the abra. At that time we would park our cars by the abra area and then get the boat across.

Land prices back then were very cheap. Later they became higher and higher. People who sold their land would come back after two or three months and say they wished they hadn't sold it. The most prized land was in the *souq* – both on Deira side and in Bur Dubai. There weren't many people at that time, so everyone liked to live in the central area – in Al Buteen or Al Ras – because they wanted everything to be close. Even the biggest piece of land we sold was only thousands of rupees – not that much. In Al Rigga, land was between two and five rupees per square foot. Today it's thousands. Nobody wanted the land where Sheikh Zayed Road and the Trade Centre are now – it was very cheap.

When The Creek was dredged and more land was created along the shore the new land was sold by Sheikh Rashid for only ten rupees per square foot. It's the area that's now Maktoum Street and Baniyas Road, where The Land Department is now.

If the people of Dubai had known at that time what was going to happen, things would have been different, but a lot of people kept their money at hand and didn't want to invest in land. If only they had known the future. I know people who started from nothing here and have become multi-millionaires by dealing in Dubai's land.

Khalifa has retired from The Land Department and now has his own business.

1. Henderson says 1949 was the last year a major fleet went pearling from Dubai. Arabian Destiny, Henderson, 1999, p 74.

2. The Maktoum Bridge opened in 1962. Father of Dubai, Wilson, 1999, p 86.

CHAPTER 15

Sheikh Rashid with Abdullah Saleh

The Banker

ABDULLAH MOHAMMED SALEH

I was born in Sharjah in 1942 – I worked it out from the Islamic calendar and I think it's fairly accurate. I remember as a child if we wanted to come to Dubai from Sharjah to see our relatives we would come by boat across Khan Creek in Sharjah and then take a donkey to Dubai. It would take about an hour.

I first joined the British Bank of the Middle East (1) as a trainee in the mid-1950s. At first I either stayed with relatives in Dubai or went back and forth from Sharjah in a taxi or a pick-up to work – sometimes hanging on to the sides. We didn't think it was that adventurous at the time – it was more adventurous drinking the water really!

The bank had opened in Kuwait and Bahrain and came to Dubai because there was business here. We had a community, the Bastakis, who had come from the Lingah area in southern Iran and settled in the Bastakia area. (2) A lot of people in Deira became rich during the Second World War by dealing with Iran and the neighbouring states. It was through smuggling rations of sugar, tea and rice – people here took them to Iran and made a lot of money. There was a lot of trade in Dubai. It moved here from Sharjah because Sharjah Creek was silting up and nothing was being done about it. Dubai was also more liberal.

The first branch of the bank opened on The Creek in Deira in an area known as Times Square – it was in Al Ras, at the narrowest point of The Creek and where we used to cross. The building had a windtower and its lavatory was well-known as it stuck out over The Creek. Once there was a miscommunication and the slit in the lavatory was mistaken for a post box by someone delivering post in the bank. The letters fell directly into The Creek and had to be retrieved from the water! (3)

I remember when Dubai was more of a village than a town, when the only means of transportation across The Creek was by *abra*. In those days the *abras* didn't have engines, they were rowed across. If you were at a party on the Dubai side you had to be aware that by 10 o'clock the *abras* had mostly gone. Some *abra* men would charge you twice as much as normal or more to get home. You had to look after them in the daytime so they would come to your rescue at night. One *abra* rower I remember was Khamis. I used to look out for his lantern through the darkness and shout out his name and although he was far away, when I identified myself he would come to transport me. There were occasions though, when I had to put my *kandoura* on my head and swim across with the fish nibbling me – I remember that well.

'For those who were used to having their money to look at and touch every morning, it wasn't easy to trust a bank.'

Banking was a little bit primitive to start with and we had to be careful not to upset our customers. Asking them how much money they had would mean the end of the relationship – it was not thought to be the bank's business. Even if I asked who a person's business partner was – although we knew – I would still get a 'not your business' answer. We had to be very sensitive in our handling of customers. It wasn't the kind of banking we were trained to do – where a person signed for something, we verified the signature and the transaction took place. The culture was totally different. We had to do 'Bedouin Banking,' so to speak. (4) Some people would send their man with a little chit saying, "Please give so-and-so 5,000 cash," which was a lot of money in those days. You didn't know whether to give the money or not. I used to take it myself to the customer and if he was having lunch, I'd have to sit and have lunch too. Still he wouldn't understand why I didn't give it to the man who'd brought the chit.

We would carry money in trunks from the Sharjah branch and I would drive the Land Rover while my cashier sat next to me. A guard would sit in the back, sleeping most of the time – we didn't even know if his gun would work or not.

A lot of people kept their money at home. Coins were buried in the sand – maybe some are still there. It was a question of trust. For those who were used to having their money to look at and touch every morning it wasn't easy to trust a bank. There was interest to be earned, but a lot of people didn't take it. (5) The real catalyst was if money was stolen. A lot of houses were made of *barasti* so it did happen. People then realised it was safer to keep money in the bank. We had to show them the vault to persuade them the money was physically safe. Of course a lot of the money wasn't there, it was invested, but there were stacks of money for people to see.

Dubai was always open – people were respected regardless of their origin, colour or religion – Hindus, Christians, Muslims – Shiites and Sunnis. I remember the incident during the war between India and Pakistan when there were some clashes here in Dubai. Sheikh Rashid told the groups to stop fighting. He said, "Listen, you are not Indians and Pakistanis here, but locals. As long as you are working here you have to forget your background, otherwise, don't stay. Fighting will not be accepted." Ever since, that feeling has continued.

Dubai went through a period of, shall we say, 'Trade with India.' There were goods – gold and silver coming into Dubai. A lot of Indians were here, importing and exporting to India. That was an interesting era. There was a feeling of gold fever. We were not a country – the UAE was not in existence then. Dubai was a free port, there were no restrictions and people would buy goods to re-export them. There was no control over those activities. The rulers here were very liberal – it was different in other states, but here there were no restrictions as long as you were

I would go to Sheikh Rashid's *majlis* in Jumeirah in the evening and around nine o'clock he would pick up the phone to the Zabeel Palace gate and say "Asha" – "Dinner." It meant Sheikh Rashid was on his way. For some reason, there was a new policeman who wasn't briefed. He answered, "Shu asha?" – "What dinner? This is Zabeel – are you mad?" and put the phone down. Sheikh Rashid laughed – you would never upset him with that sort of small incident.

a law-abiding person. If you made money it was yours, the government didn't interfere with the business, there was no red-tape and, in fact, protection was always provided.

I met Sheikh Rashid properly for the first time in 1958 at his big house on The Creek. An English man from the RAF base in Sharjah had had a car accident – he had reversed, hit a woman and was in the bank too afraid to come out. There was a local gentleman making a lot of noise, but I calmed him down. The woman was sitting on the ground, but she was alright. I went with the English man to the ruler to explain what had happened. The first thing Sheikh Rashid asked me was whether I was from Bahrain, because of what I was wearing – Bahrainis used to wear suits too. I told him I was from here – precisely from Sharjah. After I'd explained the situation, Sheikh Rashid said I should tell the man not to worry and the chap couldn't believe how nicely he had spoken. I think he'd been expecting to go to prison, but this was Sheikh Rashid – he was always like that. He had a natural talent – he looked into your eyes and would know if you were talking the truth – if you were intelligent, a good businessman or not. Sheikh Rashid asked the businessmen in his *majlis* to consider the idea of starting a local bank. The thinking behind it was commercial – BBME played a very big role in helping Dubai, but it had a monopoly so it could dictate what was in its interest. Commission was high and it was even controlling some trade so to break that position the establishment of another bank was needed. The National Bank of Dubai opened in 1963. A Scottish man, David Mack, was the General Manager and the board left it to him and me to run the bank.

We were consulted on a lot of issues. When the pound was devalued we had to try to calm people down; the same when India decided to withdraw the rupee. India was worried about what was happening to its currency because of the gold smuggling – if rupees earned through smuggling were surrendered to the bank here, the bank could then ship them to India in return for foreign exchange – sterling. When the Indians decided we had to find our own currency Abu Dhabi opted for the Bahraini dinar and we chose the Saudi riyal. Later that was superseded by the Qatar and Dubai riyal. (6)

In the beginning there was no central bank and no currency board. I went to London to see our notes being printed myself at the De La Rue company. When I went there currencies were being printed for Iran, Saudi Arabia and some African countries. At the time we printed the currency the 500 dirham notes were considered too high a denomination to distribute. For three years those notes were stored on the third and fourth floor of the National Bank of Dubai – of course they were not issued so had no value, but gradually we were told to release the money into the market.

For me it is a source of joy and pleasure to remember how we started and where we are now. A lot is forgotten and people try not to mention or remember it, but this was reality and this was our life.

Abdullah is the Vice Chairman of EmiratesNBD.

1. Originally the Imperial Bank of Persia, the bank opened a branch in Dubai run by the British in 1946. Its name was changed to British Bank of Iran and the Middle East and later to British Bank of the Middle East or BBME. It became part of HSBC in 1999.

2. See Chapter 5, 'The Pearl Merchant'.

3. Edward Henderson, writing about the late 1940s, says the lavatory was the most prominent toilet he had ever encountered and certainly a landmark. Arabian Destiny, Henderson, 1999, p 68.

4. See Chapter 21, 'The Industrialist'.

5. Islamic law prohibits the charging or payment of interest.

6. 1966. See note on currencies in introduction

CHAPTER 16

The Provider

NOORAH SULTAN FARHAN MUBARAK

WITH TRANSLATION ASSISTANCE BY HER DAUGHTER, DANA ABDULLAH

I was born in 1947 in Al Rifaa in Bur Dubai. Our house was about 20 feet long and 15 feet wide and was made from dried palm branches. Living there was me, my mother, my grandmother and my grandmother's sister – all in one room. My father's room was separate.

My father was a captain of ships which meant for one month he was at home and then for three or four months he was away at sea. If he was going far away he went on a big ship – like the ones you can still see on the Deira side of The Creek. The boats were owned by merchant families like Bin Dalmook and Al Amlah. My father went from Dubai to Africa, Yemen, Zanzibar, Malabar, (1) Bahrain, Kuwait and other countries. They carried rice, sugar, clothes – lots of things. When I was small I used to listen to my father's stories about all the places he visited. Once, when he had been away for a long time I didn't remember him when he came back. I saw him and said, "No, he is not my father." I thought my uncle – my mother's brother – was my father. My father was very angry.

When I was seven I went to the *muttawaa's* school where we first did the *Juz Amma*, the beginning of The Koran, and then the whole Koran. We learned how to pray, the Hadith, and all about the Prophet Mohammed. If people were clever they went there for one year and would finish. I finished The Koran after two years because I wanted to play too much. The

'There was no choice about leaving school, I had to earn money if I wanted to eat.'

muttawaa was good, but I was naughty and I was beaten with a stick. There were maybe 20 boys and girls at the *muttawaa's* house. Boys sat on one side of the room and girls sat on the other. We read The Koran three times from the beginning to the end.

When we finished we had a party and we gave the *muttawaa* special sweets and money. We went around the streets to the families of the boys and girls in the class, then to the ruler's family and the neighbours. They gave us coins and money. We wore special clothes – a green dress with a special *shayla* with silver in it and also a necklace, earrings and bracelets. The celebration started in the morning and went on all day.

Next, we went to learn stitching and *talli*, which is like embroidery and is sewn on dresses for decoration. Sometimes the embroidery took 20 days or more to make for just one dress.

After that I went to a government school. It was Khawla bint Al Azwar School (2) in Al Shindagha – just behind Sheikh Saeed's house. It was the best time in my life and I still love Shindagha today because this was where I was happiest. At the start we wore our own dresses, then after a year they gave us a uniform – at that time, everything for school came from Kuwait. We learned how to read and write, mathematics – everything. It was a very happy time for me.

I didn't finish my schooling – I left when I was 12 because my grandmother became sick and couldn't work very well. I had to go with her to work in another family's house. There was no choice about leaving school, I had to earn money if I wanted to eat. I made a stall outside our house to sell things to people and children going by. We made a table out of wood and we bought the things wholesale from the market and sold them; beans, dried yoghurt, sweets and so on. Also, I brought some children to our house to teach them The Koran so I became a *muttawaa* myself. If the children were good, they didn't need the stick, but if they were naughty they needed discipline – just like I had needed it before!

In the 1960s I went to work at Dubai Airport as a security guard. (3) It was the old airport with only one building. I earned 400 Qatar and Dubai riyals a month at that time. I was checking the passengers in the women's section. Some women would try to take knives or guns on the planes to give to their husbands, but we told them it was forbidden.

'Some women would try to take knives or guns onto the planes but we told them it was forbidden.'

I remember Sheikh Maktoum's wedding. Everybody was talking about this wedding – he was one of the ruling family. A group of ladies – about 10 of us – went from our area. It was the first time I had ever seen a video camera. There were many different dances and lots of celebrations. It was a little far from our house, but we went everyday for a week – everybody in Dubai celebrated this wedding. People came from the Deira side by *abra* and we either walked or ran to the place. We went to see for ourselves what was happening.

There were only two Dubai ladies working in the airport at that time. The uniform was trousers, a blouse and a hat, but I wore my own *thoub* and *shayla* – my grandmother didn't want me to wear a uniform. Some people gossiped a little about me doing this job, but they knew I didn't have anyone to give me money. I had to earn it. By then my father was staying in the house not working and he wanted to eat. My grandmother too. If I wasn't working, who would bring food for them?

Al Hamdulillah, when *Ittihad* happened things changed for women like me. We got the chance to work in the ministries, the hospitals – anywhere. Sheikh Zayed gave ladies the freedom to work and to be equal. We were so happy because our life had changed. I went to work at the Ministry of Public Works. Everything was good. We worked, we got a good salary and everything for our families became easier. We were helping to build our country – the men and women together. First there were women teachers and doctors and women went into the ministries – now there is a lady in the government. (4) The start of the UAE made an enormous difference to my life. At the time of *Ittihad* we felt the Emirates had one hand and one heart and nothing would come between them.

Since 1981 Noorah has been a teacher at the Dubai Handicap Centre where she instructs children and young adults on cooking and housekeeping skills.

1. Malabar coast, Kerala, south west India.
2. The first girls' schools were established in 1958; Al Khansaa in Deira and Khawla bint Al Azwar in Bur Dubai.
3. See Chapter 17, 'The Aviator'.
4. Sheikha Lubna Al Qasimi.

The Aviator

MOHAMMED A. ALKHAJA

I was born in Dubai on 17th March 1950 in Naif Road, Deira. I went to Al Ahmadiya School – the old one and then the new one when it moved location. At that time Kuwait assisted the Dubai government with education which meant when it came to high school we physically had to go to Kuwait to do the high school exam. I was one of the last people to do that before the Dubai Government took over education here.

My father was a businessman importing things from India and he didn't have a very relaxing life. He was one of five brothers and two brothers were always in India. They would take it in turns to go between Bombay and Dubai and their boats would cross in the middle of the ocean. It wasn't an easy life.

My father told me he used to see the flying boats landing on The Creek, but he said he didn't know what they were or why they were there. I learned later that Imperial Airways started flying to Dubai in 1937 on the way to Australia via the Indian Subcontinent – mostly for postal services. They used to pay ten rupees to land the aircraft on The Creek.

In 1959 Sheikh Rashid ordered the building of an airport and it opened in 1960. The first airfield was where the Cargo Village is now. It had 1,800 metres of runway, an apron and a terminal building with a small fire station. When I was at school I used to persuade my great uncle to allow his driver to drop me at the airport in his Land Rover and I would do my exam revision next to the control tower. The area was only four kilometres away from town, but it was quieter than being in a busy house. I was an aviation-minded person from the beginning.

If I was ever lucky enough to see a plane, of course I left my books to go for a closer look!

Most people of my generation stopped education at the high school level – there were no scholarships and everybody wanted to work because all our fathers were business-minded. My philosophy was a bit different. While I was at high school I started learning English on my own – from Indian teachers on the Bur Dubai side. I would cross on an *abra* in the afternoons, study English for an hour and come back. It cost 20 rupees a month for the teacher.

Like now, students were seconded to government offices during the school holidays and I was the only one who wanted to go to work at the airport. It was 1966. Because of the financial difficulties in those days I decided to continue working after the secondment and on 18th June 1967 I officially joined Dnata at Dubai Airport as a clerk. I was the 24th staff member. I worked in the afternoons and continued my high school studies in the mornings.

At first we only had a day operation – from sunrise to sunset. At that time there were not many aircraft coming through Dubai. Excuse me for saying it and it seems strange now, but at sunset we, as the handling agents, would just lock the airport and go home – there wasn't anything else to do. The terminal was very simple. It was white with a transit lounge, a cafeteria, an immigration office, a small customs hall and up next to the control tower there were four rooms for the air traffic controllers, navigators and other technical people. There was also a small cafeteria outside for passengers and by 1968 the duty free shop had started, but it simply belonged to private people who rented a space in the transit lounge.

My starting salary was 375 Qatar and Dubai riyals a month. After three months I got an extra 25 and for every course I passed, another 25 as a merit. As a job, I thought it was good – it meant I could afford to run my personal affairs rather than depend on my father – importantly I could pay for my English lessons myself.

When we were working there was no question of how important you were, the fact was an aircraft had landed at Dubai Airport and it had to go on schedule. People were very committed. If an aircraft came, we all worked – everyone did what needed to be done. When I was shift leader we had only one vehicle to pick up all the staff, porters and so on for work. If the driver was sick I had to go to collect them myself.

When I joined, Dubai Airport was handling light aircraft like DC-3s, Doves and so on with a maximum of 32 seats. Mostly they were on regional operations to the Gulf, Bandar Abbas and Bandar Lingah. We also had flights between Dubai and Al Ain because the road journey was very difficult – there weren't flights to Abu Dhabi because people went overland. Towards the late '60s we started to have larger and larger aircraft. Some airlines started operating DC-7s mostly for cargo and DC-6s which had a maximum capacity of 65 passengers.

Now, don't ask me about the security in those days! For example, we didn't have x-rays before the baggage was loaded. The passengers boarding any flight would just walk out to the aircraft. Falcons were taken onboard and daggers were very common among Omani and Bedouin passengers. Some people would bring guns and the ammunition had to be removed before they boarded. There were no security checks like now, but everyone liked each other in those days. It was very friendly and nationality and religion didn't matter.

'...at sunset we would just lock the airport and go home – there wasn't anything else to do.'

When the operation became 24 hours at Dubai Airport small jets started operating which carried just below a hundred passengers. I believe it was in late 1968 when BOAC (1) Comet 4Cs started flying via Dubai. It was because of the location, the uplift, the refuelling and the winds in the area. With an extension to the runway and more modern navigation aids, a year later BOAC started flying VC-10s through here on their way to Australia and New Zealand. The VC-10s were the most comfortable aircraft in those days and it was a big revolution in aviation in the Gulf that Dubai could handle these aircraft.

113

Dnata didn't have a training department so we had to depend on the airlines to help train us. The BOAC airport manager selected me for training and I went to London in 1969. Bearing in mind where I'd come from, it wasn't easy to go to a big city. I'd never seen a bus for myself let alone sat in one and suddenly I had to get across London alone. I had no contact with my family while I was there because we had no telephone at home. I did call my manager at the airport – he lived opposite my family in Deira so he passed on the message that I was alright.

Sheikh Rashid's decision to increase the length of the runway and build a new terminal, which opened in 1971, meant

BOAC flights used to carry pets sometimes and messages would say, 'Dog on board, hold number two – please feed and exercise'. Once this happened and I checked with the loader it was done. He said it had been a huge dog, but that all was fine. After two days BOAC contacted us to say a dog had arrived, but not the same dog. They said a black dog had left London, but a brown dog had arrived in Australia. We double-checked and told them that everything had been alright leaving Dubai. Eventually the loader owned up. He told us, "When I opened the hold the dog was so huge it had broken the cage. It jumped over me and ran off into the desert and I couldn't chase it over the runway." He had got the watchman's dog, put it in the cage and sent it to Australia! I never did tell BOAC – I don't know if there's still a claim.

more airlines started coming here. When war unfortunately broke out between India and Pakistan that year, the airlines that had used Pakistan moved to Dubai.

After more training I was given the task of starting a cargo department in Dubai from scratch. We didn't have storage and there were huge cargos coming in at this time because the country was developing so much. The demand was so high we built 30 warehouses.

I worked at the airport with my two best friends, Mohammed Ahli and Ismail Ali – people used to call us The Three Musketeers. We became qualified for everything on the ground, but the government also wanted us to know what went on in the air. We attended a three month technical course in the UK and when the first flying school opened in Dubai the Three Musketeers learned to fly. We were the first three UAE civilian pilots and we flew between Dubai, Abu Dhabi and Ras Al Khaimah.

Emirates Airline came much later – it was in 1985 that the government decided to launch an airline. I was among a small group of about five senior people who worked to start it. My job was to set up the overseas stations. We only had a few months to complete everything. We were very excited, but the most excitement came when our aircraft took off. The Ruler, Sheikh Maktoum, Sheikh Mohammed, Sheikh Hamdan and the other VIP's boarded for a flight over Dubai. When the engine started and I saw the tail of our aircraft with the emblem of our flag, tears of happiness came into my eyes because it meant that my country was going to be visible everywhere and everyone would know us.

Those in aviation say being an aviator is something in your blood – it never goes away. When I think back to doing my homework under the control tower and watching the planes, I realise how lucky I was to be able to join Dubai Airport and Dnata. I can now see where aviation has reached and I know that my decision was correct.

Mohammed is the Senior Vice President for Safety and Standards for the Emirates Group. His fellow musketeers, Mohammed Ahli and Ismail Ali Albanna are Director of Operations for the Department of Civil Aviation and Executive Vice President of Dnata, respectively.

1. British Overseas Airways Corporation – successor to Imperial Airways and forerunner to British Airways.

The Falconers

SALIM RASHID SAEED AL MAGAOUDI

TRANSLATED BY HIS FRIEND, SAEED SUWAIDAN SAEED AL QAMZI

DEMAITHAN SUWAIDAN SAEED AL QAMZI

TRANSLATED BY HIS BROTHER, BUTTI SUWAIDAN SAEED AL QAMZI

I was born in Deira in Murshid in 1946. My father went diving for pearls in the summer and in the winter he was a falconer. I joined the *muttawa* for three months and did half the *Juz Amma* before my family moved to the desert. When I was young I helped my father and my brother. We brought wood from the desert to sell it and also grass for the camels and cows.

I learned about falcons when I joined Sheikh Rashid's entourage. I was around 14 years old then. Before, there was hunting by camel, but by the late 1950s we went by car. We used to go from Zabeel out into the Dubai desert towards Al Ain or Hatta. We also went to Ras Al Khaimah and other places – with cars we could go further and we caught many houbara bustards. We would go hunting and camping for two weeks at a time. Between 20 and 30 people – some of Sheikh Rashid's friends – would go on the hunting trips. Then Sheikh Rashid started to hunt further away – he would take a boat to Iran and the group would stay for around two months at a time. There were many houbara bustards there too.

I was with Sheikh Rashid as a driver and a falconer at this time. I would drive a Land Rover on the hunts with eight people in the back on seats which went down the sides of the car. Sheikh Rashid's Land Rover had around six people in the back and the Sheikh in the front with his driver. I had my own falcon for hunting. There were three front seats in the Land Rover and my falcon sat on its *mingella* in the middle one. The co-driver held his falcon on his arm.

In the camp the Sheikh's tent was at the top of an oval ring of tents and nearby was the windbreak made of wood and grass, with a fire in the centre. It protected us from the wind and also from scorpions and snakes. It meant everyone could talk in one circle together. Sheikh Rashid would sleep in the same tent as his close companions like Hamad Bin Sougat, (1) Salim Bin Salim, and Khalifa Al Akraf. The Sheikh's sons had their own tent and their own companions.

We would get up for *Fajr* prayers around five. There were groups hunting here and there with the Sheikhs until around 11 o'clock when we would cook and eat lunch. In the afternoon

'There was one man who was very specialised in sewing the eyelids of the falcon when it was first caught...'

we would go hunting again and come back to the camp before sunset for dinner. If we had caught many houbara, everyone ate them, but if we had only caught a few birds they would be cooked for the Sheikh and his close friends only. The others would eat sheep which we would buy from people who lived in the area.

We would talk about the hunting news from the whole day – how many houbara had been caught, who had lost their falcon and which falcons had been beaten by the houbara.

We lost many falcons. We might have started hunting with 30, but sometimes we brought back only ten. The falcons would track the houbara for many kilometres and some would get lost behind the dunes. In Dubai we never got lost ourselves because we knew the area, but in Iran and later in the 1970s when we went to Pakistan, people got lost many times and had to sleep away from the camp. The Sheikh knew we could manage by ourselves though – we were men. Once when it was very cold, one group didn't have any covers under which to sleep, so they built four fires – one in each direction – and slept in the middle of them. Later we had wireless radios so we could send a signal and if it wasn't picked up the others would look for us the next morning. They knew which area we were likely to be in.

I went to Pakistan to trap falcons. We used a pigeon as bait and caught the falcons with a net. There was one man who was very specialised in sewing the eyelids of the falcon when it was first caught, to calm it down and prevent it breaking its feathers. He would sew very carefully from below the eye to above the eye and then tie the thread from each side on top of the falcon's head. New falcons were taken to this man. It was a very delicate job putting the threads in and taking them out.

Falcons are in my blood. It's traditional and I love it very much. Whether I have been poor or whether I have been rich I've always loved to be with falcons. Before, I drove the Sheikh's car, but now I have three four-wheel drives of my own. Still my falcon sits with me in the middle.

I was born in Zabeel in 1966. I am the youngest of five brothers. My father was a special guard for Sheikh Saeed and Sheikh Rashid. I saw my father with falcons – he loved them. His father too. This love was passed from grandfather to father to sons.

Before, people here relied on falcons to help them catch things to eat. Back in the time of my grandfather and before, the life was hard. There weren't weapons to shoot food and one falcon could feed several houses. There was a bond, a love, between the falcon and the man. Our father would tell us our falcons were part of our family and that we must look after them. If a falconer has five children then the falcon will be the sixth. If he loses his falcon, he cannot sleep. If my falcon is sick then I am sick.

I went hunting with my father from a very young age. Sometimes I would not go to school, I'd go hunting instead. I would tell my mother my face was dirty because I'd played sport in school, but really I'd been hunting!

I remember my first falcon. I hunted hares with it and it was very good at catching them. Now the situation has changed and hares are rare, so if you hunt them you will go to prison for sure. That first falcon was with me for four years, then I cut its rope to let it go wild for breeding. For the falcon, this is very good. If you loved a falcon you had to do this. If you kept it, you would reduce the number of good falcons in the world. Before we released the falcon we would feed it very well to make sure it would be alright even if it didn't find food straightaway. When some people set their

'One of the best places to trap wild falcons in Dubai used to be Ras Al Khor, at the top of The Creek.'

falcon free they cried – it was their baby, but we had to remember it was for the future.

One of the best places to trap wild falcons in Dubai used to be Ras Al Khor, at the top of The Creek. The falcons came from the northern Gulf and they had followed the seabirds. Anywhere along the coast where there were small creeks or channels and where the small birds were, that's where the falcons came. The islands offshore were a good place as well.

Whenever I had a new falcon, I wouldn't be able to sleep because I was so worried about it. From the early days I have kept my falcons with me while I slept. The second day after I was married I took the falcon into my bedroom to sleep! The falcon for Bedouin people is something that is so special.

We were born as hunters. My father would tell me I shouldn't catch more than I needed for myself and my family. He would say if we didn't need to kill an animal, we shouldn't – one hare was enough for two people. Before, if we went hunting we would share what we had caught with our neighbours – it meant there was fresh meat for everyone. By the 1970s hunting was a habit and a sport, but it wasn't needed for food. People worked during the week and went hunting at the weekend. They would sit around the fire, chatting and remembering 20 or 30 years ago when they had caught this bird or that bird.

One of my funny memories was when my father was training his falcon and it flew straight into him and hit him on the head. I turned around and I couldn't see him because he'd fallen down. The falcon was fine, but my father was only thinking about his bird – when you are a falconer, you don't think of yourself, only of your falcon.

Salim and Demaithan (known to his friends as Sheaba) fly their falcons whenever they have the chance during the season. They often meet with their fellow falconers at a majlis *in Zabeel.*

1. See Chapter 4, 'The Loyal Companion'.

CHAPTER 19

The Volunteer

AMINA IBRAHIM AHMAD

TRANSLATED BY HER FRIEND, FATMA MAJID AL-SARI

I was born in Deira, in Dubai, in 1958. Our house was made from date palms. My father worked at sea for most of this life as a *saib* and then a pearl diver. Later he was involved in the traditional dhow races. I used to see my parents helping each other – if my mother was cooking my father would help her. They didn't marry because they were in love, but later they did come to love and respect each other. There wasn't divorce like now – people didn't have problems like today and they wouldn't divorce for just any reason. Life then was very simple.

First I went to Fatima Al Zahra school in what is now Al Rigga Road. I remember the first time my mother brought me to school. I was seven and I started to cry. My mother told me if I didn't go to school she would take me back home and put my head down and legs up and hang me upside down! I felt very small – I was seven, but some of the girls were 15 years old. Everyone brought their daughters to the new schools because they wanted them to be educated. My mother was not educated, but she knew it was good for me to go. When I started studying in school the books, the clothes and the shoes were all from Kuwait. There was a green uniform with checks and later we wore a white blouse and blue skirt. Everyday we had breakfast paid for by Kuwait. The teachers were Palestinian and Egyptian – they were like mothers to us.

'My mother told me if I didn't go to school she would take me back home and put my head down and legs up and hang me upside down!'

Later, when I was 11, I went to Amna bint Wahab School in Deira which is where the Dubai Women's Association is now. I have been with the Association since I was a young girl.

I got married when I was fifteen years and completed my studies in the afternoons. The morning was for the unmarried girls and the married ladies studied afterwards.

When I was younger we would go in a big group to Fujairah or Ras Al Khaimah for a week or two weeks between school times in the spring. Everyone would camp together and share their food. This was our fun.

We went to live in an area called Al Manama which is now known as Hor Al Anz East. There was a big fire there so people also used to call it Al Muharraq which means burnt. I remember that fire, I was about 11 years old, and it was a blind man who started it. He wanted to cook so he lit a match and put it in the kerosene. There was an explosion and the whole place caught fire. At that time the houses were made only from wood and palm fronds. More than 15 houses were destroyed, but thank God nobody died. We had to take what we could and leave. The government moved us all to a special camp in the Abu Hail area and gave us sheets and crockery and so on to start our life again. Afterwards they gave us houses.

In the 1960s I took my mother to the houses where Hessah Lootah and her friends had set up groups and classes. (1) Then, in 1976, I began volunteering at the Dubai Women's Association. At first I was still studying, but on Thursday I would finish my cooking early in the morning and come to help. In the early days everyone would volunteer because they wanted to help and make something for the people of Dubai. We didn't have any money, but we gave from our hearts and helped the Association grow. We would help people who needed money or clothes and if we heard about problems in other Arab countries we would collect money and send it to them. When there was a problem, we tried to help.

The Association was very important for the ladies because before it, they didn't have a place to go – not like the men who had their clubs or the *majlis*. We had some courses like nursing, typing and photography. Afterwards many of the women got good jobs – in the Ministry of Health or one as a photographer in a national newspaper. Some of the women who studied here in the 1970s have become today's leaders in Dubai.

My husband is from the same area as me. I used to see him when I would go to his family's house, but he was ten years older than me so I didn't think we would ever be married and at that time he didn't think we would be either. We didn't fall in love before we wed.

There was no engagement party, but the wedding party was very nice. The men were outside the house and the women inside – everyone was invited and we gave food in dishes to the other houses in the area. My father didn't come to the wedding though because it is our tradition that fathers show sadness when saying goodbye to their daughters. We had five dances performed; it was usual at that time because it was very cheap to have them – we gave only 1,000 dirhams for these five dances. My husband gave me 6,000 dirhams for a dowry – before marriage he gave me 5,000 and 1,000 he kept in case there was a problem in the future.

We didn't go on a honeymoon, the traditional thing was for the bride to stay in her mother's house for a week with the bridegroom. Some people had started to go on a honeymoon by the time I got married in the 1970s as there was more money – they would to go to Bombay or Lebanon and later to London. Before then it had been difficult to travel because people had to get special papers. Then we became one country and everyone had the same passport – a UAE passport. After staying in my mother's house for one week I was taken to my husband's house. I remember my mother started to cry, but the houses were not very far apart. I was her only child though and it was a big change for her – and for me. Before, my mother had taken care of everything for me and when I went to my husband's house I started to clean, cook and take care of everything for my husband and for his family's house. My husband's mother taught me. I was only 15 years old – I didn't know anything. We lived all together in one house. I learned to remember the good things and keep back the other things. This is life.

'If you didn't get pregnant after one month of being married people would start talking.'

If you didn't get pregnant after one month of being married people would start talking. Sometimes mothers would push their sons to take a second wife. For seven years I didn't have a baby. The hospital told me this is something from God. Now, Al Hamdulillah, I have six children. I remember my first daughter got such special things from my friends because she was the first child after many years. Life is very sweet.

Amina continues to volunteer at Dubai Women's Association where she is a media co-ordinator.

1. See Chapter 13, 'The Determined Scholar'.

CHAPTER 20

The Migrant

ZAKARIA DOLEH

If it is true, I was born in Jaffa in Palestine in 1927. I was in Kuwait from 1948 and I first came to Dubai in 1965. I came here for a visit, liked the people and the place and I decided to stay. Now I have Emirati nationality.

The area where I live, Al Hudeiba, was all palms when I first saw it. There were wells with sweet water – much of the water that went on donkeys to the rest of Dubai came from near here. The story given to me was that my plot had belonged to one of the most wealthy merchant families, but things had changed and they were selling it. I bought it for a quarter of a rupee per square foot in 1965. My estimation was if it was worth one rupee by 1970 I would be more than lucky, but in 1967 it was already worth two or three. Things started from there. My house was built in stages. At first I built a hut with wood I brought from Lebanon. Then I brought oil drilling pipes and put the hut on top, among the palms. There was no planning, no drawing – I created it from my own style. For the roof I took the measurements from a poster of a Japanese house. People started saying my house was a church, that it had ghosts, many things, but I didn't care. One Lebanese architect told me it was out of place, but which building here is in its place? If we stuck to what belongs here we'd still be living in barasti huts!

I came to Dubai as a foreigner and I didn't know anyone. A man became my friend through a deal – he was very close to Sheikh Rashid and suggested I went to the *majlis*. For years I regularly went with him. I had no official designation, but it was nice to be in a place which was like a school – everyday there was a new lesson.

The beauty about the people here was that they weren't spoilt by money. Sheikh Rashid didn't give them money, but he gave them the chance to make it. I believe Sheikh Rashid was born to rule. He didn't need power to rule – people loved him. One Bedouin asked him, "Sheikh, what's your secret? If we ask for something from you and you give it to us we are happy. If you don't give it we are supposed to be angry, but still we feel happy." That was the secret of him.

I remember a German-Arab friendship delegation came in the 1960s. I speak German so I translated for them. In the morning we went to see Sheikh Rashid at the *Diwan* to say hello and in the afternoon to a villa in Jumeirah (1) which was like the parliament. The German man asked me, "Does Sheikh Rashid believe in democracy?" I had to translate. Sheikh Rashid then asked me, "Did he need permission to come?" It was as though he was laughing. "What more democracy is there than coming to the ruler and sitting down without an appointment?"

Arabs generally didn't like figures and time keeping, but Rashid did. He had a big influence on the attitudes of the merchants here. He was always on time. He was a man with brains. No matter what the reality was you had to tell the truth.

He would stare into your eyes. He would trust you, but he would check you. If he told you to be somewhere at four o'clock in the morning, he would be there before you, to make sure of you. The minute you weren't committed, you'd gone – he'd turn his face. That created people of responsibility. To work with sheikhs is not an easy job. You are trusted and you must do what's to be done.

In Sheikh Rashid's time Dubai had no money, but he had the foresight to borrow money. If he'd waited until we had oil to build what he had in mind it would have been too expensive. He put in all the infrastructure – it was a high price at that time, but very cheap for today.

His wife, Sheikha Latifa, had a beautiful saying which I know from my wife. She used to say, "If a tree does not give fruits, cut it from the bottom." In other words a palm must produce – mankind must produce. Here, it is a desert – you don't grow decorations – you must have realistic thinking. Sheikha Latifa was proof that every great man is supported by a great woman – that is what she was.

When the oil money came it went on hospitals, schools, the police and so on. It didn't go for palaces – Sheikh Rashid had a very humble life. He loved Dubai and there was a devotion inside him. Also he loved success. People who understood his mind and horizons did well for Dubai and made their own fortunes. There is nothing wrong with that.

Dubai is a transit place. Sometimes people say it's smuggling, but it is not, the business is re-export. I noticed that for merchants here the property was like a safety factor – it's part of the economic system. The merchants bought the land and slept on it. It's like an insurance. You can always sell it, but the merchants didn't unless they needed to. I would always tell a particular friend of mine he should buy land and he would say, "But Zakaria, the Arab desert is so vast." I still managed to sell him several lots. He told me lately, "One of the lots you gave me for 25,000 in the 1960s is worth around 100 million now."

I went hunting with Sheikh Rashid to Iran and Pakistan. Hunting with falcons is in the sheikhs' blood, but I calculated that if you go to the supermarket to buy one frozen pheasant it would cost 10 to 15 dirhams. If you went hunting it would cost 1,500 minimum for one houbara – the aeroplane, food, the pocket money and so on! I looked at it from a business point of view.

'Here, it is a desert – you don't grow decorations – you must have realistic thinking.'

The beauty about hunting is you wake up before the dawn, drink coffee, smoke, have breakfast and then you're on your way. I went in Sheikh Rashid's team. The first time I thought we were driving to the end of never. I didn't know how we would get back. I was so scared – I thought we were lost, but it was an illusion of my mind. Others in the group

131

When Sheikh Rashid died, he left a great gap in my life and I was very scared no-one would carry the message of Dubai onwards. Luckily the young fellows have inherited his strength. Life goes on. I wish from my heart that he was alive today to see what Dubai has become. I see it for him now. I have no doubt this is what he wanted for this city. He would love Dubai as it is now.

knew exactly where we were – somehow. The Land Rover was rigid – if you weren't used to it, you were bumped about. There is a technique, like riding a camel, and you must move in the same direction, but it still hurt. I learned the hard way.

During hunting, everybody was a friend. We cooked when we were out during the day and Sheikh Rashid would come to stir the pot and check on the lunch.

I used to think the entire hunt was done by the falcon, but that's only a small part of the deal. It is the Bedouin who see the prints. They can tell if they're fresh and which direction the bird went in. When they found fresh prints they would follow them till they led to the prey, take it by surprise and let the falcon go.

At the end of the day, we came back to the camp and the talk was of what had happened during hunting, whose falcon had caught the most, the competition, stories, teasing and so on.

On one trip, after three days Sheikh Rashid came to me and told me to take my belongings. I went in the car with him back to the palace which was three hours drive. I became really worried. I asked him, "Your Highness, did I do something wrong?" He told me, "Don't be foolish, go back to Dubai – the market there is very hot." He knew I was a businessman first and foremost.

'I love to see a place, see if something can be done and watch myself and the place grow together.'

Dubai is a business atmosphere. I've never had any dispute. I like to start from scratch in a place – it is a habit for me. I love to see a place, see if something can be done and watch myself and the place grow together. No-one here has shaken hands with me and made losses – they've all made money and I've made money as well.

Zakaria is the Director of Dolphin, a real estate, contracting and general trading company. He lives in Al Hudeiba in Dubai surrounded by his children and grandchildren.

1. Now Union House on Jumeirah Beach Road.

132

CHAPTER 21

The Industrialist

OBAID GHANIM AL MUTAIWIE

I was born in a village called Jumeirah which stretched along the sea. It was the 1950s and the houses were small and made of *barasti*. There was no electricity, no water, no sanitation. People lived a very simple life. My family has lived in this area for more than a hundred years. We lived from fishing and pearl hunting and my uncles and my father had a number of boats.

In the summer very few people stayed in Jumeirah because they wanted to move to a drier climate. It was very humid by the sea and there was a lot of fungus because there was no sanitation, so people would lock their *barastis* and go on their way. Some people went to Al Ain as water, fruits and dates were available there. Back then, both societies – in Dubai and Al Ain – lived on what they harvested during winter. Jumeirah people caught fish in winter and preserved it with salt they collected by donkey from the end of The Creek. They sold the fish and bought dates which they brought back to Dubai by camel and lived on for the following season.

Before, there were no banks so people hid the money they earned from pearl hunting underground, in clay pots. You didn't know if a person was rich until he was dead. (1) My father told me they had Marie Theresa coins made from silver, but that if you kept them under ground, they became greenish and scaly, so every year people would cook them with dried lemon in a pot over the fire. They did it at night and in secret so no one would see. The head of the family would bury the pot and that meant if he died people didn't know where the coins were buried. This happened for so many families including ours when my uncle died.

By the end of the 1950s and early 1960s people had started bringing cars here such as the old RAF lorries called Bedfords. They would take them to Al Ain over the dunes as there were no roads. One year when we hired a lorry with other families from Jumeirah we were half way to Al Ain when we had an engine jam. I remember they took all the water from the radiator, cleaned it and gave it to the children. It was a hard time, but people made ends meet and nobody grumbled. If you were short of something you'd go to your neighbour and get food from them. Life was so sweet and so harsh at the same time. People were very close – they shared what they had and helped each other.

There was an electricity generator in Jumeirah, I think it was in the early 1960s, and I used to start it. I would get there at 6 o'clock, put in the diesel and start the generator for the Jumeirah Number 1 area. The houses had only one bulb for each room.

When the oil was discovered in Saudi and Bahrain my father and uncles went there – people went to where there was work. Many of our people in Jumeirah went to these other Gulf countries.

In the 1960s Dubai started progressing with lots of trade and big projects. The city was built by Sheikh Rashid piece by piece, and things started to change here. There was the airport, the dredging of The Creek, a bridge from Bur Dubai to Deira, roads and later the deep water harbour which is now called Port Rashid. Business really began then. That was when people started making money – it was the turning point for Dubai. I remember when we realised that Dubai had struck oil at sea. It was 1966. Helicopters dropped pieces of paper to congratulate the people. Those who had gone abroad to work started to return.

Huge tanks called *Khazzans* for storing the oil at sea were built on the beach in Jumeirah by a company called the Chicago Iron and Steel Company. They dug a lake where the Madinat

Jumeirah is now, built them there and then tugs towed them to the oil fields. They were enormous tanks which had to settle in the ground in deep water. Still they are using them now. (2) Later, a hotel was built nearby – where the Jumeirah Beach Hotel is now and it was called the Chicago Beach Hotel.

I did my apprenticeship at British Petroleum in Abu Dhabi. We were still in the Trucial States, but there was good co-operation even though the UAE hadn't been formed by then. We were taught English and engineering and then we went to Das Island on the border of Abu Dhabi, where all the oil installations and rigs are. Later I went to Bahrain and London and after I graduated I returned to Dubai. It was 1976.

I was so lucky. Sheikh Rashid had started another of the big projects in Dubai – the Dubai Dry Docks. This was the big turning point in my life. It was Ramadan and the new Jumeirah was being built. They were distributing houses for the locals for free, but they gave you what was available at that time – without thinking if you had a big or a small family. I had a big family, but the man who was distributing housing refused to give me a big house, so in the evening, at Iftar, I went to Sheikh Rashid.

I said to him, "Your Highness, you are the ruler. I have been working hard and learning in the UK and have brought you back a good education and this man wants to give us the smallest house in the town! I don't want it – I want a big villa!" It was the first time I'd talked to Sheikh Rashid. He said he would give me a big villa and I went back to my brothers to tell them, but they asked how I expected to live in a big villa with them living only in small town houses. I had a big problem. I went back to Sheikh Rashid the next day to say, "Thank you, but actually now I need six big houses for all my family!" He was very, very generous – he gave me the houses and he told me he wanted me to work with him at the Dry Docks. He spoke to somebody there and I got the job.

I was working for the Sir William Halcrow company on the mechanical and electrical engineering installations. The piling of the Dry Docks was just starting when I joined and there was a lot to be done. It was a great experience for me and I worked with many engineers and architects – people I could learn from for the future.

As I could speak Arabic, and also because he had given me the job, I was the one who had to report to Sheikh Rashid every week in the *majlis* on the progress of the Dry Docks. It was nerve-racking as I wasn't very experienced back then. Often the *majlis* was full at the time I went and he would ask difficult questions so if you weren't attentive you were in trouble! I had to be very honest. There was no point in trying to make things sound good. He would go to visit the sites of all the projects in Dubai including the Dry Docks to make sure there was

no difficulty or delay. After six months of going through this 'training', as I would call it, we knew each other better. What he wanted to know was whether things were going well and on schedule. If there was a problem he would ask me to bring the people from Halcrow to explain.

Much of the infrastructure for Dubai was built between 1973 and 1980. These really were the years of construction. My friends and I felt we were a part of something big. By 1979 many of the projects initiated by Sheikh Rashid were nearly at an end. The Queen of England was invited to open Jebel Ali Port, the Trade Centre, DUBAL, DUGAS and of course, Dubai Dry Docks. A lot of the work had been done by British firms – Cementation, British Steel, Costain, Taylor Woodrow and Halcrow were all involved and there was some financial help from Great Britain.

In the last months before her visit we were working day and night to finish our project. Close to the opening Sheikh Rashid came to the Dry Docks three times one day. He told me, "Please, make the Queen happy". Sheikh Rashid had a great sense of humour. For the opening of the Dry Docks we had a big circular platform where the Queen, Sheikh Rashid and all the VIPs were to stand. Then the Queen was to press the button, the platform would turn 98 degrees,

'suppose this Obaid didn't build the platform well and the Queen and I fall down into the dock?'

the pumps would start and the water would begin pouring into the dock. Humaid bin Drai was the protocol person and he was very agitated because the Queen was coming. Sheikh Rashid wanted to make him more nervous. He said, "Humaid, suppose this Obaid didn't build the platform well and the Queen and I fall down into the dock?" Humaid was so nervous wondering what would happen if the Queen fell down. In the end everything went well. It was a huge project, everybody was watching us – we couldn't afford for it to go wrong. All the hard work paid off. Dubai had had the courage to generate many projects and it was a success story. The people who were part of it will never forget that time.

When the Dry Docks were finished Sheikh Rashid called me and said, "From tomorrow, you will be going to the Dubai Ship Docking Yard at Jaddaf as Chairman." It was a big shock for me as I was only around 30 years old. I went from being an engineer to the Chairman of the Board. It was a responsibility, but I just had to get on with it.

Obaid is the Chairman of Al Mutaiwie Investment Group which has interests in manufacturing, trade and construction. He still lives in Jumeirah with his family.

1. See Chapter 15, 'The Banker'.

2. *Khazzan* refers to the Arabic word for storage. They were 90 metres wide, 70 metres tall and the shape of inverted champagne glasses. The area in which they were built became known as 'Chicago Beach'.

CHAPTER 22

The Horseman

ALI KHAMIS AL JAFLEH

I was born between Dubai and Abu Dhabi, almost on the border, so some documents say I was born in Abu Dhabi and some say Dubai. Anyway it doesn't matter as long as I was born in the Emirates. We are one of the oldest families and we come from the Liwa area, west of Abu Dhabi. We still have a lot of family there. I am over 40 years old, but less than 50. I did my early schooling in Dubai and then I went for the rest of my education in the UK. After that I joined the government's service.

I would say in the 1940s and 50s there were no such things as 'jobs' in this part of the world. People like my father were living by their own business – importing things from the desert to sell and then buying food from the city to take back to their families. Then there was a season when they went to sea, for diving. My family had its own boat which belonged to us. The captain was the oldest brother and the rest of the crew were his brothers and his son-in-laws – all the family.

My father used to ride horses and I would see the horse and camel saddles in the house. I don't think they were Pure Arab horses he rode, because in those days it was hard to get a Pure Arab. Perhaps they were crossbreeds.

Our family joined the Sheikh to be part of his people, his security and, let's say, his friends. The Sheikh helped people, fed them and in return they were loyal to him. My father believed that

Sheikh Rashid was a fine leader and a great person. There was a tribal war and they fought together. They were protecting the area from intruders. Where Sheikh Rashid used to go, my father would go with him. When Zabeel Palace was built, we moved to Zabeel.

We feel we are the sons of the late Sheikh Rashid. He was the man behind all of us – brothers and sisters. I was so close to him that sometimes I felt I wouldn't know if he was my father or Khamis was my father. My father, he loved Sheikh Rashid dearly. When we ate something, he would always say, "God give Sheikh Rashid a long life. Pray for him." My father died very soon after the death of His Highness. He just couldn't take it.

I learned to ride on a pillow. My father used to let me sit on a pillow and he would put a 'rein' in my left hand. He would say, "Don't move the horse by pulling the rein left or right, just use your knees and lean to the left or to the right."

When we moved to Zabeel the stables were around us and there were lots of horses. We had one barn and 20 small boxes for the horses, no air conditioning. I could be wrong, but the weather at the time seemed a little bit kinder than now.

The horses were very hard and tough, but luckily they were not fast. We could manage to stop them and turn them. I used to see Their Highnesses, Sheikh Maktoum, Sheikh Hamdan, Sheikh Mohammed and Sheikh Ahmed riding. I rode mostly with Sheikh Ahmed because we are the same age. We were so enthusiastic to see the horse, ride the horse and challenge each other. We raced between the dunes and we were glued to the horses. When we saw a horse tire, we would take it back to the stable to change it for another. We had started riding without saddles, but then we got Arabian saddles – they were soft and you could hold on. We had learned the difficult way and become better.

In the late 1970s, I had been going back and forth to London for some time and I used to enjoy reading 'Sporting Life'. (1) I couldn't tell between grey and bay at first, but I started going to the racecourses at Epsom, Ascot, Sandown, Windsor and so on with a group from Dubai to see racing for myself – and to learn. Every year I went racing I enjoyed going to the steward's room as an observer. That's how I built up my knowledge.

By the 1980s I was thinking, "If they have racing in England, why can't we have racing back home?" Of course I am not a man who takes decisions, but I thought I would be glad to take part and help. The Maktoum family took a decision and said, "We will race." Their Highnesses were interested in bringing horses from abroad to sell at a good price to encourage people to participate in the competition in Dubai. A lot of local Emirati people bought the horses at first.

To start with there was no quarantine and nobody worried which horses came and went from the country – any animal could walk in or out. Then we became aware that horses could come with diseases and so the government took a decision to seal the border, with the help of the Ministry of Agriculture. In the early 1990s we did a survey all over the country to clear the horse diseases from wild and loose animals, like camels and donkeys. One trip, I went with the government vet to chase the animals and let me tell you, when you chase donkeys on the dunes it is very hard to stop them! We were supported by the army. We found a big number of loose donkeys and we checked all of them for diseases. There was only one reported, an old male donkey so we found a home for him. There was no other disease.

I believe Nad Al Sheba was built in the early 1980s. When I joined, in the early 1990s, the grandstand was basic, but it had room for over 700 people plus VIP seats. That was great for the old days. When it comes to the Nad Al Sheba of today, you're talking to a person who was part of the group that put the bricks together. His Highness, Sheikh Mohammed, gave instructions to develop the grandstand, the racecourse, the track, even the car park – everything necessary for racing.

'By the 1980's I was thinking, "If they have racing in England, why can't we have racing back home?" '

The first meeting at Nad Al Sheba was in 1992. Sheikh Mohammed was there. I think we had six races and would you believe it the first one or two were raced by crossbreeds. Then there were one or two Arab and two Thoroughbred races.

There was an old track in Al Ghusais which I saw before the airport started expanding. It was 2,400 metres or one and a half miles long and it was a round shape, not oval. The winning post was exactly by the grandstand – it must have been built by someone who had a background in racing, perhaps by the British.

The ground was *sabkha* with no grass or sand. I saw a footprint of a horse – *sabkha* holds footprints for a long time. The grandstand was two storeys and I, myself, counted about 120 places people could sit on the concrete. In the middle the VIPs also had an area. It looked like there was a parade ring and paddock. I asked people in the area and they said they used to race camels and horses there.

The thing I remember most about it though was that I was worried. The night before, I swear I didn't sleep. We had rehearsed the stalls and the photo finish, but I was still worried about an electrical failure. I was also worried whether people would attend or not. There was no betting, but we wanted people to be part of the sadness and happiness of racing. I think there were maybe a couple of thousand people in the end.

In the early days we had a press conference, but the next day hardly anything was written in the newspapers. The next week I told the press, "A day will come when you will have an edition for sport and another edition only for racing."

Most of the people involved in racing in the beginning had a background in the sport in Europe and Asia, so if we said there was a stewards' enquiry, then they understood it was a stewards' enquiry. If we said the horse was last, it was last. This made life easier most of the time. Sometimes though we would disqualify a horse and the owner would come to ask why. We'd say, "Sir, your jockey deliberately obstructed the other horse and kept him on the rail in order to win". The owner would say, "Well then you should punish the jockey and let my horse keep the winning place!" We'd have to do a lot of explaining about the rules! From day one Sheikh Mohammed told us, "Don't give an inch, go by the rules and don't worry about anything." It's got a lot bigger now, but it was difficult work then. It's like the Burj Al Arab. It has a foundation smaller than the whole building, but the foundation is still important for the future. The foundations that were laid in the early days mean racing in Dubai and the UAE can now reach the sky.

'...Sheikh Mohammed told us, "Don't give an inch, go by the rules..."' '

Ali's love of horses continues and he enjoys race meetings in the Emirates and around the world whenever he is able.

1. British sporting publication.

CHAPTER 23

Juma Al Majid and foreign visitor with Sheikh Rashid

The Merchant

JUMA AL MAJID

I was born in Shindagha, in Dubai, in 1930. Our house was built from stone and gypsum and all the family lived in it. I went to a *muttawa* for school. Most of the people in the Gulf worked in pearl diving. My grandfather and my father were in this business – people trained their children for the same work. From the age of nine I went with my father.

Most of the families in Dubai had at least one boat for fishing, travelling and pearl diving. Our family owned two boats. My father was the *nokhada* on one boat. I looked and learned from him – I opened the shells and helped on the boat. Our servant was the *nokhada* on the second boat. Servants were treated like family, not as servants – they ate together, sat together and worked together.

The work of pearling is the hardest work I have seen in my whole life. The divers were in the sea for the whole day and the *saibs* would stand all day to pull them up. Now, even without work, people can't stand the whole day.

When the pearling season was over everyone came back to Dubai together. They had to wait for the signal – a flag being raised by the leading captain to say everyone could go home. That was the rule so the crew couldn't put pressure on the captain to return early from this difficult work. Everyone in Dubai was happy when they came back safely – the divers had been away for three and a half months. When the boats returned people used to stand and clap from the shore.

The *tawawish* would come to our house. My father would sell his pearls to the highest bidder, but he wouldn't show the pearls to all the pearl merchants; he only showed them to a limited number, so as not to spread the secret of the price until they were sold – afterwards people knew. (1) Sometimes the *nokhada* had the power and sometimes the *tawwash* had the power depending on the demand in the market around the world. Sometimes the *nokhadas* were forced to sell their product to give their workers money – some wanted to go back to their country; some had come from Oman and some from other countries. My grandfather told me that before, our people went from here to Ceylon (2) to dive during the British colonial times. The British government would make the boats ready for them and check before they went they had no knives to open the shells. When they came back, before the shells were opened, they would divide them – half for the British government and half for the divers. Then the British would put the shells in an auction for people to buy. If people wanted to put their shells in an auction the British would do it for them too.

Pearling in the Gulf was in the summer. In the winter my father would either take goods from country to country by boat or he would go to Jebel Ali to fish for sharks and sardines – he fished mostly from the shore. Then, when the cultured pearls were produced in Japan the demand for our pearls declined and the Gulf went bankrupt. The weight of the pearls – a *chow* they called it – had been 2,000 rupees, but it fell to 70 rupees. People here didn't know why the price had gone down and pearl diving was the only way they knew how to make their living. We had a good life when

'...when the cultured pearls were produced in Japan the demand for our pearls declined and the Gulf went bankrupt.'

the value of the pearl was very high and we faced a hard life afterwards. Before, the people in the Gulf had surplus money – the people not the government. When the public is bankrupt though people must find another way to live – they had to find different work.

Some of the divers would work in the airport in Sharjah (3) for very little money each day. Some of the people who had bigger boats went to Iraq, Iran, India or Africa for trade. My father's boat was not so big and we remained poor. I remember it was a very difficult time. The fishing boats didn't have engines then, only sails and they would have to go far out to sea. Sometimes there were big storms and there were occasions when boats would sink in the middle of the sea.

In the Second World War Dubai was under British control and the British helped by bringing food into the area. Each family had a ration card to get food depending on how many people there were. They got flour, tea, sugar and rice – if there was rice available. The British did a good thing. The poor people didn't want to use tea – it was a luxury. They wanted to buy dates and flour so they sold the tea and sugar back to the shops and the shops sold it to other people who smuggled it to Iran. It was not allowed by the British law. Some rules are correct, but some rules are not to the benefit of the public. When they are not, it is not good.

I had moved to Deira with my family and around 1947 I opened a textile shop in the Old Souq. The textiles came from different areas, but my uncle, Ahmed Al Ghurair – my grandmother's brother – gave me about 700 rupees capital in goods. The shop belonged to them and I started from there. They had a big boat to go to Africa and India and bring the goods – Saif Al Ghurair, his son, was in India and sent goods from there. (4) He had been a ship's captain since he was a teenager.

Local people came to my shop as well as people from Oman and Iran. I would buy goods from the local market and I paid for them weekly. Every Saturday the traders would come around to collect the money in the shop and I would pay part of what I owed them – they trusted me so they would let me have the goods before paying for them.

People from different places were involved in the gold trade. It was not only Dubai people – Indian people, English people and others took gold to India. Some foreign banks in Europe used to send their gold with the merchants in Dubai – on their account without even a letter of credit or a bank guarantee, such was their trust with the people in Dubai . The merchants would sell the gold and send their money back to them. Nobody lost. Now, nothing can be done without a letter of credit, but in those days people were trusted with billions.

I was there when Indira Gandhi came here and asked Sheikh Rashid to stop the gold smuggling. He told her we had no smuggling because Dubai was a free market. He said everybody sells gold and that her people came, bought gold and took it. Gold is not something that is harmful to humans. It is business – people benefited from the gold because it was purchased at a cheap price and they became rich. Even now people buy gold from here because it's cheaper and take it all over the world.

Dubai wasn't like other places; it was a free place and very open for trade. This has been the secret of Dubai until now. There was respect for people involved in business and the law was very strict and correct.

This history is our history – and we have to talk the truth.

Juma is the Chairman of the Juma Al Majid Group which deals in construction, general trade, travel and financial investments. He is the founder of the Juma Al Majid Heritage and Culture Centre in Deira.

'This history is our history – and we have to talk the truth.'

1. See Chapter 5, 'The Pearl Merchant'.
2. Sri Lanka.
3. The airfield in Sharjah was used from 1932 by Imperial Airways. RAF Sharjah opened in 1940. See Chapter 10, 'The Migrant Worker'.
4. See Chapter 7, '*The Nokhada*'.

THANKS

We have eaten breakfast, lunch and dinner, taken coffee and tasted dates with the tellers of the tales in this book and we are grateful to them for allowing us to be their guests – in the present as well as their past. We are indebted to both the storytellers and in many cases to their families and friends for the enthusiasm displayed and the trust which they placed in us. Thank you also for the belief and conviction that these precious memories should be shared with a wider audience as well as being handed down for future generations to wonder at; you took a chance for which we – and your grandchildren – will always be grateful. In some cases the tales of one individual alone could have filled a whole book so we apologise if not every detail and recollection could be included, and thank you for your understanding.

To the trusted translators a special note of thanks, particularly for their patience and attention to detail with the checking and double-checking of information and meaning. We are grateful to you for having the courage to tackle often personal and difficult issues and for explaining seemingly ridiculous questions to your friends and colleagues. Many people made helpful suggestions about individuals who might be fascinating to talk to and happy to be included. Chief among them were Rashad Bukhash, Abdul Khaleq Abdulla, Magda Ahmed, Abdulla Abdulrahman Al Rahma, Michelle Sabti, Maha Gargash, Dr Mohammed Hamdan, Mike Simon, Mona Hauser, Hamad Mohammed Bin Mejren, Dr Ebtisam Suhail Al-Kitbi, Dr Nadia Buhannad, Ron Hinchey, Safiya Burnell, Yasser Mabrouk and Mohammad Al Murr.

For smoothing the way and making things happen, thanks to Ursula Musch, Sultan Butti Bin Mejren, Major General Sharafuddin Sharaf, Captain Salem Bin Hendy, Warrant Officer Khalid Al Mazroui, the Dubai Police, Obaid Khalifa Budahum, the Dubai Women's Association, Osman Aburuf, Khalid Aziz, the Dubai Department of Tourism and Commerce Marketing, the Heritage Village, Al Ahmadiyah School, Dubai Dry Docks and Jens Larsson.

We are particularly grateful to Dr Hasan Al Naboodah, Associate Professor at the UAE University's Faculty of Humanities and Social Sciences whose unerring enthusiasm and support went well beyond that which we might have hoped for. For his deep knowledge and willingness to share it, our thanks to Abdullah Hamdan bin Dalmook. For their specialist expertise we would like to thank Dr Obaid Butti Al Muhairi, Peter Jackson, Dr Anne Coles, Jack Briggs and Anthony Bubb.

To all the colleagues, PAs, secretaries and assistants who were repeatedly pestered in our determination to speak to and photograph their bosses, we apologise and thank you for your understanding.

Thanks to Imelda Dunlop and Doug Mackay for their considered feedback on parts of the early manuscript; to Tilda Bowden and Wendy Pascoe for their ideas and support; and for her early suggestions and later understanding, Katy Donaldson. To Lyn Bicker, for being as confidence-building and positive as she has always been and to Alan Bicker for his valuable suggestions as well as for being the anthropological pedant he loves to be.

Thanks to everyone at Explorer Publishing for their energy, professionalism and commitment to the book from the first time it was suggested; particularly Alistair MacKenzie for prizing enthusiasm so highly, Pamela Grist for always finding a solution that worked, Pete Maloney for his wonderful creativity and patience and Claire England for her good sense and sheer stamina in editing.

Thanks to Claire Bernardino for always being there, to Geeta Krishnamoorthy, Paul's secretary, for organising his life and to his assistant, Kalu Thapa, for being ever at the ready.

Finally, thanks to our respective spouses Kirtie and Steve for their consistent belief in us. Words cannot express how good that feels.

RESEARCH BIBLIOGRAPHY

Father of Dubai, Sheikh Rashid bin Saeed Al Maktoum, Graeme Wilson, Media Prima, 1999

From Trucial States to United Arab Emirates, Frauke Heard-Bey, Motivate Publishing, 2004

On the Folklore and Oral History of the United Arab Emirates and Arab Gulf Countries,
Selected and Edited by Adnan K. Abdulla and Hassan M. Al Naboodah,
Zayed Center for Heritage and History, 2001

Arabian Destiny, Edward Henderson, Motivate Publishing, 2002

Mother Without a Mask, Patricia Holton, Motivate Publishing, 1997

Arabian Sands, Wilfred Thesiger, Penguin, 1991

The Maktoums and Their Horses, Volume 1, Edited by Graeme Wilson, Media Prima

The Distinctive Arab Heritage, A Study of Society, Culture and Sport in UAE,
Dr Ahmed K A Al-Mansoori, Emirates Heritage Club, 2004

Don't They Know It's Friday?, Jeremy Williams, Motivate Publishing, 1998

www.sheikhmohammed.com
www.usc.edu/dept/MSA/reference/glossary.html
www.islamicbanknotes.com/gulfrupees%20(article).htm

GLOSSARY

A

Al Hamdulillah
Praise be to God

abaya
robe worn by women, usually black

agal
twisted black cord which keeps *gutra* in place

areesh
woven date palm fronds for building structures, also name given to houses made from the fronds for summer living which had a loose weave (to allow air to circulate more freely) and flat roofs

Asr prayer
afternoon prayer

ayyala
male celebratory dance performed at weddings

B

barasti
generic term for structure made from date palm fronds

bayt al shaar
literally 'house of hair', traditional tent made from sheep wool and used by Bedouin in winter

burqa
traditional mask worn by women made of a stiff textile

C

chow
unit for weighing and valuing pearls

D

dana
a very good pearl also known as a *hasbah*

dhow
type of boat

Dhuhr prayer
midday prayer

Diwan
Ruler's Court

diyyin
container to collect oyster shells from the seabed

E

Eid
Muslim festival and celebration

F

Fajr prayer
dawn prayer

fatam
peg made from bone, clipped on the nose for diving

G

ghaff
type of tree found in the desert

girba/girab
leather container/s for food and water

gutra
headdress worn by men

H

habban
traditional instrument made from goat's skin

hasbah
a very good pearl also known as a *dana*

Hajj
muslim pilgrimage to Mecca

I

Iftar
breaking of the fast during Ramadan

imam
religious leader

Isha prayer
evening prayer

Ittihad
federation or union, the United Arab Emirates came into being on 2 December 1971 with six emirates as signatories, Ras Al Khaimah joined in 1972

J

jus
gypsum plaster

Juz Amma
part of The Koran

K

kandoura
dress

khaimah
literally 'tent', also name used for houses made from date palm leaves that had a tight weave and pitched roofs for winter living

khanjar
dagger with curved blade

khazzan
seabed storage tank for newly-pumped oil

khizam
special type of *agal* worn by Bedouin (and Dubai's first police officers)

M
Maghrib prayer
dusk prayer

majlis
meeting or meeting place

maktab
Koranic school in a house taught by a *muttawa/muttawaa*

mingella
carrier or perch for falcon

muttawa
literally 'volunteer', term used for teacher at Koranic schools

muttawaa
female 'volunteer', as above

N
naham
singer

narilla
pipe for smoking made from coconut shell

nokhada
captain of a boat

Q
qarat
Arabian gum tree, an infusion of its fruit was used by pearl divers after diving and the wood was used for boat building

R
Ramadan
Muslim month of fasting

S
sabkha
type of soil, salt or mud flat

saib
hauler, the person who pulled up the diver by his rope when he felt the diver's tug

samar
type of tree, found in the mountains

sanbouk
type of boat, often used for pearling

Shariah
laws of the Islamic religion

shayla
head covering worn by women, usually black

sheikh
title used for member of ruling family, religious leader or wise man

sheikha
title used for female member of ruling family

shisha
large Middle Eastern smoking pipe

sirdal
head captain of the pearling fleet

souq
market

T
tajir
merchant, some of whom went to sea as *nokhadas* in the pearling season

talli
very intricate decorations on the neck, cuffs and trouser cuffs of women's clothing

tawwash/tawawish
pearl merchant/s – who did not go to sea for pearl diving

thoub
dress

towi
water well

W
wezar
sarong-like garment worn under men's *kandoura*

Y
'yalla'
'let's go', informal expression

Z
Zakat
alms

TELLING TALES

AN ORAL HISTORY OF DUBAI